The Meaning Of My Tattoo

BY

Nika J.

Absolute Author
Publishing House

TABLE OF CONTENTS

FOREWORD

"It's not the load that breaks you down, it's the way you carry it" – Lena Horne

It was in the bathroom at church in Charlotte, NC that I met Nika. I was breastfeeding my daughter and I spoke to her and was captivated at how she had this young/old look about her. She had a few little girls with her and one on her hip, all the little girls were listening attentively to her. There was something about Nika that was magnetic but she also had the look of a black girl lost. She appeared to be in church as a last resort; like she had lived a thousand years and this church thing just had to work. Somehow, I knew I wanted to get to know her, not as a project but to genuinely get to know her. It took us roughly a year to really have a conversation once I joined the dance ministry and after one practice Nika and I became friends; not just church girl friends but I knew we could share our true identities with one another with no judgment. I quickly learned that she was a single mother that put her all into church, her business and most importantly her children. I learned that Nika loves hard and would give her last if you needed it. I witnessed her throw a baby shower with a 24 hour turn around for a young lady that she barely knew in her home because she got word that she didn't have anything for her upcoming baby.

Nika and I were walk buddies for almost two years and if those sidewalks could talk they would tell a lot about us. We spoke unfiltered, raw truth and most importantly honest. To me it was like a "walking diary" that was nonjudgmental. Nika spoke to me about her family structure and dynamics in detail, however, she rarely went into great detail about Teff. I knew just enough to know who he was, how much he meant to her at one time and that he was her middle daughter's father. There was always a mystery about Teff, and as close as we had become it always felt taboo to bring him up. However, I always felt that Teff had a hold on Nika even in death. It was like she needed validation, love and attention that only he could give her.

I was always aware that Nika was writing her story and that it was important to her. In all honesty it felt like Nika was blowing smoke in the air because it was taking too long to write. I have heard Nika say hundreds of times "because I'm writing my book," or "when my book comes out." On the inside I was like "would you hurry up and come out with it already." Not knowing Nika was baring her soul and getting gut honest with the ugly parts of her life. As close as I felt to her with my background in teaching and counseling, Nika had/has wounds that only time and writing her memoir could heal. It went deeper than our church talks, mid day chit chats, or even our weekly hour and a half walks. Nika had a lot of healing to do and the pages of this book is the very start that she needed to free herself from the hold that Teff had on her.

This book is gritty, raw, gripping, sexy, hood and oh so Charlotte. It is a testament that black and brown people often suffer in silence. Mental illness spreads like wildfire and it doesn't care who it affects: young, old, innocent, educated, socioeconomic background or even your gender. The stigma sticks to you and imposes its ugly ways on your being as a whole. The black and brown communities shun the notion that mental illness exists in our space. It's a tangled web that occurs in families more often than not. This is a story of triumph and what happens after the victim becomes a victor. I am so proud that my friend Nika, has come through a fire but doesn't smell like smoke.

Avis Fields
M.S. Mental Health Counselor, Director of
Diversity/Educator

INTRODUCTION

October 3rd 10:12 pm

My son is dead" Shelia stated furiously. Click.

I just sat on the floor. Not because I didn't want to get up, but because my legs simply refused to operate. Chi Chi my best friend handed me the blunt. Before I could hit it a second time, she said wearing a serious face I did not recognize.

"We gotta get the fuck outta here."

I continued to sit in the same spot on the floor with the same confused look on my face shaking my head from side to side telling myself that this is not happening. I continued to hit the blunt again and again until Chi Chi reappeared in front of me. Just realizing that she had even left my presence, I looked up at her from my gaze to hear her say, "I'm about to put this stuff in the car, get up and get in the car, I got the babies".

"Why Chi Chi, where we going?"

"Nika, the way Shelia just called and said that shit, ain't no telling what she thinking or what she might do, she might be on her way over here now, she crazy let's go".

She had an arm full of clothes and other random items. I watched her disappear behind my front door as I tried to pull myself off the floor. I had finally stood up by the time she came back in to grab Mariah off the couch. I dragged my body to the car pausing to hit the blunt on the way. Before we could back the car up, my phone rang, and I went insane. I screamed,

"Turn it off! Turn that ringer off! I don't wanna ever hear that ringtone again!"

"Hey,.......No she's right here beside me..... she's..... she's..... okay.....okay, yeah I know, I got her, I'm taking her with me now. Oh wow....really?....Oh my God! Well, she will be with me, don't worry about that. Okay hold on.

She turned and looked at me. I was already staring at her the entire time. I knew it was my daddy. He was always really loud like he was on speaker phone in his normal voice, but he was even louder this night. I heard every word. I wish I hadn't. He told Chi Chi about how crazy it was at the scene and about how he had burst through the crime scene tape to make sure I wasn't in there.

"It's your daddy". She tried to hand me the phone. I just looked at her and shook my head no.

"She don't wanna talk……yeah….right this shit is crazy". She turned to me and said, "He said he loves you".

I shook my head yes.

"She loves you too, ok, bye."

CHAPTER 1

OFF TO 8-TRACKS.

May 31, 2002

"Y'all about to leave?...... Why y'all even come if you go leave all early?"

I looked at her like she spoke another language.

"We just ready to go". Harriett my neighbor we rode with that night snapped back with a strong Ohio swing in her words.

"Aight, we ain't leaving, we'll get a ride".

I walked off with an attitude to find my cousin Kesha. I found her on the patio, hugged up with some nigga.

"Them bitches left us". I blurted out upon arrival.

"Wha? We just got here". My cousin responded.

"That's what I'm saying, I told that bitch bye".

"Right, we'll get a ride home", she agreed.

"I'll take y'all home".

I turned my head toward the dude all hugged up on my cousin. I gave him the same look I'd given Harriett.

"This is my cousin Nika, she mean as hell".

"Hey Nika", he reached his hand out for me to shake.

I just looked at it.

"Daaaaamn", he said laughing.

He turned to Kesha and said, "But yo for real, we'll get yall home, that's not a problem".

"See Nika, we straight".

"I don't know him", I said with a straight face.

"This Tony, you done heard me talk about Tony before", she explained.

I just looked at her thinking, "Do you realize how many niggas you tell me about?"

Before I could say anything, the tall drink of water I'd been eyeing earlier walked up to us. I had already eye raped every 6 foot 3 inches and 280 pounds of a man. He looked like he had been dipped in chocolate. Not to mention how the light shinned off his thick brows and thick beautiful curly hair. Then he smiled. I was weak. I looked him up and down fighting my grin with my serious face.

"This my cousin Teff, we came together".

"Cus, they ride dipped on them, I told them we'll gettem home."

"Oh yeah fa sho" says the tall drink of water.

"What's your name?" I asked.

"Teff".

"That is not your name".

He responded, "You too pretty to be so mean".

That's when my grin slipped out. Dang.

"See, that's what I'm talking about. So, you go dance with me or what?"

He flashed his big pearly whites and we grinned at each other for a few seconds.

"Yep"

And we were off.

The way we danced. The way we looked at each other while we did it. All eyes were on us. Our chemistry stole the room. We eventually returned to the patio for a smoke while the sweat dried from our performance.

"Damn, where yall been?"

"Dancing", I answered.

Tony and Kesha looked at each other then back at us smiling. I knew what they were speculating about, it was true and neither of us cared. I proceeded to plop down on his lap and ask him 21 questions.

Finally, the lights came on and it was time to go. Kesha and I whispered about who was driving and what kind of car it would be as we followed behind them to the car. We finally walk up to a burgundy, Dodge Shadow with illegal pitch-black windows and shiny hub caps, with the words "Ain't Scared" across the front window. Wow, just, wow! And guess who pulled out the keys? Teff. Lucky me. Even the interior was red AND the light in the car. It was blinding, especially after as many drinks as I'd had. I gave Kesha a look. We could talk to each other with our eyes. Her eyes said, "What the fuck", my eyes said, "Look at this shit". Luckily, he drove like he had some sense; I was really praying that he was not as drunk as I was because he didn't seem like it. When we got to my house Kesha and Tony went straight to my daughter Symone's room to be grown. Teff and I sat on the couch. We talked and talked. During our conversation he told me that he had just had a son and he was only 2 weeks old. So of course, the next question was where the mom was because she could not be too far. Flag! He then explained that he and his mom were raising him because something had happened to the baby's mom, but he would tell me about it later. I asked him his real name and where did Teff come from, he said he would tell me later. I asked him what the tattoo on his neck meant, he said he would tell me later. This nigga had a lot of "I'll tell you laters", but for some reason, he had a way of making me feel so comfortable about it. Then he would flash that smile to seal the deal. Fine ass. I told him about my 3-year-old daughter Symone, how infatuated I was with my dad and that I did hair, all the basics before I fell asleep on his shoulder.

The next day my mom and dad came over. I told them all about Teff, and that he was coming over to for me to meet Miguel, his son. They seemed un-phased due to the fact that my dad had just come home from an 8-year bid, he and my mom were like newlyweds. They were all over each other and I loved it because I had never saw both my biological parents together before. It made me feel so, normal. Teff showed up shortly after with the baby. He was indeed 2 weeks old. I instantly fell in love. Everybody loves newborns. He was such a good father. He asked could he take him to the back. I watched him feed him, burp him, and lay him down to sleep, then I excused myself to get high with my dad. As I began to walk out of my room, I noticed he had a really worried look on his face, I asked him what was wrong.

He asked" What you tell your people?"

"About what?"

"About me and the baby?"

"I just told them that I just met you and you had a little baby, and I didn't know what was up with the mama".

I also mentioned that my mom and dad were so all over each other that they did not really question me much. He asked me to sit down. Then he told me this......

CHAPTER 2

WHAT HE TOLD ME.
Early June 2002

He explained that he and the currently anonymous "baby moms" (he never stated her name) had already broken up when she found out that she was pregnant, and she had already had a new boyfriend. She and the new boyfriend lived with her mom and her mom was on drugs really bad. The baby moms needed help with the rent, so Teff came by to give her $500, only, because of his son. During that transaction her new boyfriend came out and began to pick a fight. Teff said that he tried to ignore him and had begun walking back to his car when the crazy, drug using mother came out with a gun and pointed it at him thinking he had started the fight that never happened. The baby momma tussled with her mom to stop her from shooting Teff and the gun went off. The Baby moms had accidentally shot her mom in the stomach. She eventually died in the hospital and his baby moms went to jail for murder. He explained that this was why he and his mom had custody of the baby. I had an "Oh my God" look stuck on my face the entire story. It was like a movie. I walked out the room with the same crazy look on my face and headed to the already smoked out living room area to repeat this dramatic story to my parents. My mom had the same crazy face as I had when I finished. My dad uttered one statement.

"What fucking movie he steal that shit from?"

He laughed it off to amuse my mom and I, but I could tell he was not buying Teffs' story. He didn't dwell on it because he was too focused on getting shit faced as we planned. I could bet that I would hear about this later. If the weed allowed him to remember that is.

Although Teff was rather, over the top and animated, he was quite intriguing, not to mention his smile could win me over through almost anything. A lot he said didn't make a lot of sense to me, but I didn't want to have any sense. I wanted to believe him, so I did. So, we continued to do whatever it was that we were doing for the next following weeks. We hung out as often as we could which was quite often because I had way too much free time. Whenever I wanted to see Teff he was at this motel, however, I was never invited inside. It seemed that he was never at home for me to come over, but I never questioned him. Now I didn't know much about drugs at this point well, not other than weed and as far as I was concerned weed was NOT a drug, it came from the earth. Plus, I smoked it, and I'd never smoke drugs. All I was concerned about was making sure I was as cute as I could possibly be upon my arrival. I had maybe come over 2 or three times by now and I'd never actually saw any drugs, but I was far from stupid. Well at least I didn't think I was. Stupid and naive were definitely two different things.

Teff had a lot of stories. For instance, all of a sudden he didn't have his car anymore. When I asked what happened to it, he said that a crackhead hit it and he was going to get paid a lot of insurance money. Then he asked could I take him to the chiropractor. Of course, I said yes. Anything to see him. It didn't matter that it was slap across the other side of town or that he never offered any gas money. I just did what he asked and watched the sweet newborn baby when he went to the back to get his treatments. After a while, he had finally told me where he stayed. I'd have my happy ass outside right on time.

During the time I wasn't chauffeuring Teff around I was trying to get my own shit together. I was currently enrolled at CPCC but I had basically quit because I had flunked all of my classes from lack of attendance. I was still however surviving off of my last financial aid check, food stamps and a welfare check due to me having a daughter and no child support. The apartment I lived in was based on my income which was basically nothing because my only income was only from school, technically. I did however do hair, not yet licensed but I was good at it. My clientele was up and down and had consisted of guys who had crushes on me along with my childhood friends and family. I wasn't in beauty school and instead, majoring in business because my grandma said, "Don't go to school for hair, every little black girl can do hair, do something more challenging." Well, I probably should have gone to beauty school because I was surely wasting my time. I had already changed my major for the third time from criminal justice to computer information systems to business administration because, I just wanted to do hair! I left school often because someone wanted to get their hair done and it seemed way more important to me then some boring ass class that didn't pay. I followed the money. Not to mention my daddy who had been locked up since I was about 11 years old and I haven't laid eyes on since I was 6 had just been released. Regardless of those circumstances, he was my best friend, and I was completely in love with him from our years of writing and exchanging poetry while he was in prison. When he was released, I forgot about everything! Class? What class? Every second I had I wanted to spend it with my daddy, my hero, my big buff male version of myself. It had been about 3 months since his release, so things were dying down, but now I had created a huge mess for myself. No one knew the rut I was in and that I was in desperate need of a job. I was never really too fond of the job thing, but I was smart enough to know I had to do what I had to do, so I told my dad, hook me up at his job a Winn-Dixie. He did of course.

I lasted 3 hours. I could imagine that my dad was a little aggravated with me, but he had the same attitude he had about everything when it came to me.

"Daddy, make sure you get my check."

"Nika baby, why you just leave like that?"

"That nigga go ask me to mop the floor, I don't even like to mop the floor at home".

"Baby girl, that's part of the job, he said he asked you to clean up the front and when he turned around you were gone."

"Damn Right! I applied for a cashiers position, I ain't mopping no floor, he better ask one of them high school students to mop the floor, Imma grown ass woman, just get my check, I need my check."

He laughed hysterically and repeated "My baby girl." He couldn't do shit with me and he knew it.

My check was $24. Now I was back at square one. "Tommy ain't got no job," nor future or plan to say the least. I still managed to stay level doing hair at the house. I had messed up my financial aid and needed to sort out my life.

Teff knew none of this. To tell the truth he had so much going on, he never asked me to much anyway. He had enough drama for both of us.

One day Harriett, the chick that left all early at the club, which was also my neighbor from upstairs and my smoking partners girlfriend sent her home girl to get a quick weave. I did a fantastic job of course. Afterwards she came back down to talk to me. She wanted to know why I didn't go to a salon and work. I explained that it was because I was afraid of booth rent and I didn't have a license yet. She informed me that Sonya, her stylist, had an open booth for rent and that I should talk to her. She was sure that she would work with me. I told her that I would think about it.

The job hunting was not going so well, mainly because of the fact that I didn't really want a real job anyway. Finally, I was somewhat forced to go over to meet Sonya. What a coincidence that the salon was located around the corner from the motel where I would meet Teff. She was incredibly nice and inviting. The salon was rather old and ghetto, but hey, I guess you have to start somewhere. She told me that the booth rent would be $100 per week. I was terribly intimidated by booth rent as a whole. The words "Booth Rent" were just as awful to me as the words "Bullet Wound". Some weeks I would only make $100 and it was fine, because it was all mine. Then she handed me a contract. I felt like I would be signing over my life. The pressure. I asked her what would happen if I didn't make $100. She said that then we would do commission which was 60/40. That made me feel a little better. I just had to wrap my mind around giving anyone anything. So, I did not sign the contract. I told her that I didn't want to start immediately, and I'd call her when I was ready. My plan was to make sure I had the booth rent before I started just in case, I didn't make it. Besides, all of my clients were located on my side of town, this salon was located on a side of town where I didn't know anyone but Teff. And he was definitely not a client.

Teff would call me every morning before I picked him up for the chiropractor on my house phone. I had absolutely no reception in my apartment on my cricket phone unless I laid it next to the patio window. They called my house the dungeon, it was downstairs in the back. Before we would even begin talking, he would stress that I was to NEVER call this number back because it was his sisters' phone, she was crazy and lose her shit if anyone called it back. I didn't question him, but his dramatics made me suspicious. I however always noticed that the name that popped up on the caller I.D. "Saleena Paul", but he told me his sisters' name was Tisha. That name looked so familiar to me.

Most of the time, I would pick Teff up from the old run-down motel. He had Miguel with him every day, however after 5 or 6pm and on the weekends he didn't. One day he asked me to stop by the motel to hang out with him. I was excited like he asked me for a date.

Up until this time I had cornrows in my hair only because of a bad perm that I received from my friend that caused all of my hair to break off in one patch on the side. It made my shoulder length hair impossible for me to wear without looking like a tragedy. So, I decided to cut all of it off like a boy! I had been infatuated with Jada Pinkett for years and my cut mimicked hers at the time. I put on an army fatigue printed halter top with the shortest hunter green minnie-skirt I could find.

If I could have only taken a picture of the look on his face. The look said, "Damn I hate your hair!". I looked totally different from the past few weeks, and I didn't even mention it.

"Why you do that?" I ignored him and pushed him out of the way.

"Move, you go let me in or what?"

The room was full of niggas. I sat down and pulled out a cigarette and tried to look sexy because his reaction had me feeling a little insecure about my new look. He introduced me to the fellas. They were all playing spades when one fellow offered me a drink.

"What is it?" I asked.

"Everclear," the guy answered.

I gave him a disturbed look. Now I could drink. As a matter of fact, I had a rather enormous collection of empty liquor bottles displayed on the top of my kitchen cabinets from trying a different type of alcohol every weekend. I was super proud of that. I knew that Everclear was the one I was told to stay away from.

"Yeah, its 100 proof", he explained.

The disturbed look was still on my face; however, I was no punk. I reached my hand out to grab the cup that was offered to me and took it down then chased it with my cigarette.

Oh, you got you a solider," a guy I later learned name was Brad yelled, extremely impressed.

They all saluted me as they do in the army as a way to acknowledge my attire. It was cute and I liked the attention. As the fellas played spades and talked trash, Teff wrote me a note.

Him: When you go be my lady?

Me: Is that what you want?

Him: You no it, but I have one problem.

Me: And what is that?

Him: How you go be my lady, but you don't please me the way my lady should.

Before I could respond, the guy, they called A.B. said;

"Hey red, watch this."

He poured liquor all over the table they were playing cards on and then strikes a match. Teff stood up and yelled,

"Gone head with that shit A.B.!."

This dude dropped the match and set the entire top of the table on fire. I screamed and climbed backwards on someone's bed with my shoes on. Then he asked me if I wanted another drink.

"I don't want that shit no more."

They all thought my reaction was hilarious. I hate niggas. Teff asked me to come with him outside to sit in the car. We sat in the back seat and immediately he began to kiss on my neck.

I just bluntly said "I ain't fucking you in this car."

"Why not?"

"Cause, people can see us."

"So, what, you my lady right?"

I had the stupidest grin on my face that read "Yes I am".

He continued to do nasty things to me to turn me on. I had become quite bothered.

"I don't wanna fuck you in no car Teff!"

Next thing you know I was giving it to him right there in the backseat of my indigo blue Neon. I was officially his lady, and I was the happiest chick in America.

He called me from another number the next morning. The caller I.D. read "Shelia Gonzalez" this time. Gonzalez, I thought, what Mexican's phone is he using? He gave me the same warning as the first number and insisted that it was his sisters phone, again. Whatever Teff. He had asked me to meet him at 8 tracks. No problem, I was going anyway. So, I began the routine: shower, get dolled up...blunted up...liquored up...party buddy over...then the phone rang. Of course, It was yours truly, Teff.

"Hey baby, listen, don't go to the club tonight, I'm sick. Me and Miguel coming over."

"Teff, I'm already dressed and my homegirl already over here we about to le..."

This dude hung up on me. I told Big Sherry what happened. Big Sherry was Moes baby mama, a friend from high school. She stayed in the building beside me.

She was like, "Man fuck him, let's go", so we headed out.

I hadn't been there a full ten minutes when I looked up and saw no one other than the number one stunna; Teff. He was dancing hard too, sweaty and everything. I could have shitted on myself. I think my heart stopped for two or three beats. I nudged Big Sherry.

"There he go".

"Yo you lying".

"No look bitch, right there in the middle".

I lit my cigarette so fast. I could not believe this.

Big Sherry whispered loudly, "You want me to shut it down?"

She really could. Her name was Big Sherry for a reason, she was big like Baby Dee from Friday without the afro puffs.

"Nah, chill, let me see what the fuck is going on first."

This dude looked dead at me, caught eye contact with me and acted like he didn't see me and preceded with his dancing. Okay, I thought, he wants me to show out, but I won't. What to do? What to do? I had to do something. I absolutely could not let him get away with playing me like this. I felt like an idiot and I was on fire inside with disbelief and betrayal. I told Sherry to follow me. We began to make our way through the crowd. I made sure I made it up to where he was. He was about to walk right passed me. The way we walked up; he had no choice but to pass us without doing something obvious. I looked up at him as he pretended to look over me (he was 6'3). I looked down to see that he was holding another girls' hand!!! You should have seen this chick. I looked her up and down with judgement and disgust. I noticed everything. Her hair was sadly pulled back into a ponytail, barely making it. Her dress that she decided to wear with sneakers was a dingy gray. The sneakers were out of shape, and I think they were white at some point. No earrings, no lip-gloss. What dumpster did he find this bitch in? You could tell that she didn't mind fighting because she clearly had nothing to lose. She looked at me like she wanted to cut me, and I looked right back at her like I would cut her back. I had to stop Big Sherry from actually doing it!!! We went outside to the patio. Big Sherry gave me this look that said, "What you want me to do? I was speechless!!!! I couldn't do anything but shake my head and chain smoke cigarettes. I was way too confused and not to mention shocked to think of what I should do next. Next thing you know one of my home girls from back in the day walked up to me and said, "Hey girl, question, don't you mess with Teff?"

I just looked at her thinking, why are you asking me this now, and how do you know anyway?

But I answered, "Yeah, why?"

She said "You see him with his baby mama? ".

"What? His what?" I dropped my cig, stomped on it and walked nonstop directly to my car. Big Sherry was right behind me.

I was very upset, but I refused to cry. The entire car ride was silent except for my Pastor Troy c.d. I blasted the entire trip. Big Sherry attempted conversation; I turned the music up louder. Besides, my mouth refused to open because it would only allow the tears out. I should have known that I liked him too much too soon for any of this to be the least bit perfect. I was beyond disappointed, because he had told me such a horrendous lie, and I'd actually believed it, although it did remind me of a movie I'd watched before. I even told my parents. I felt like an idiot. Was I stupid? I guess I was for him to think he could tell me that lie. Guess I'll take my stupid ass to bed. So, I sadly did.

CHAPTER 3

BOOBOO THE FOOL.
Mid-June 2002

The next morning, I woke up to my home phone ringing off the hook. I did not put my cell phone beside the window before bed, but I was sure to have a full voicemail box. The caller I.D. read Saleena Paul and Shelia Gonzalez repeatedly. I'll pass. However, my very best friend Chi Chi called also, so I called her back. She wanted to smoke and catch up, so I invited her over. I told her that I had major dirt to tell her about this dude I'd met, and she was dying to hear it. We sat in the smoke area in my dining room. I began to spill all the details from the Teff files as she rolled up. She laughed hysterically. After all of the beans were spilled, we decided that instead of me staying angry that we should simply turn him into a project, somewhat of a mystery game to solve. I quickly grabbed a sheet of paper so we could jot down all the facts.

Well, I still didn't know his real name. So I wrote;

Teff

When he calls it either says;

Shelia Gonzalez

or

Saleena Paul.

Who were these women? He would say that both were his sister, but they were clearly two different people.

The name of the motel was where he spent most of his time was **The Royal Inn on Nations Ford Road.**

*His home address was **555 Cherry Stem Lane***

That was all we had to work with. So, the first thing we did was look the names up in the phone book and write down the addresses. Then we looked on the map to see where in town it was.

We found that the address for Saleena Paul was the address I picked him up from which was walking distance from the hotel. However, Shelia's address was on the other side of town. Confused. That name Saleena Paul continued to baffle me. I had heard it before. I decided to call in for reinforcement, Kesha. She reminded me that Saleena Paul was the name of a chick that went to T.A.P.P's (school for pregnant teenagers) with us, she was pregnant at the same time. Bingo! It finally clicked. The chick at the club! Saleena Paul! His baby momma! I knew it! I knew something wasn't right because of how finicky he was when I picked him up from his house. He never had the baby after 5 or 6pm, I was picking him up from HER house while she was at work. They lived together! Everything made sense now. Wow. I had been so played. I was super pissed.

So, when he called again, I was ready!

"What Teff!"

"Hey boo, what you doing?"

"I know good and damn well you don't think you go talk to me like that bullshit didn't happen!"

"Listen boo, I know you mad".

"Hell yeah, why you lie to me and say yo baby momma was locked up?"

"But she is locked up boo".

"Teff, come the fuck on".

"Boo, I didn't lie to you, see, she got released for Father's Day because she about to be sentenced. They gave her ten years, but she gone now."

Click!

This nigga must really think I'm "BooBoo the fool". I had no more words for this craziness. He continued to call repeatedly, and I continued to ignore him. Meanwhile I was busy printing flyers for my braiding prices and put them on all the telephone poles and inside of the windows of all the stores on that side of town so I could gain some clientele. A few days later I received a call from Teffs friend Brad. He asked if I would come over to the room and braid his hair. I did need the money, however, I immediately felt like it was a set up produced by Teff. So, I asked,

"Where Teff? "

"He outside".

"Call me when he dip".

Click.

A part of me did want to see him. Well, rather for him to see me only to ignore him while I was looking good enough to eat. I had no desire to negotiate anything less than the truth. However, maybe if he sees what he's losing, the truth would find his lips? Probably not, but I was going to give it a shot and make a few dollars while doing it. You know, two birds.

I proceeded to get all dolled up so I could arrive before he "dipped", when the phone rang.

It was Brad, whispering, "Hold up don't come yet".

"Whyyyy I'm already...."

"His baby momma over here, just hold up a min".

"I'm coming to get you", Click!

My heart was racing. I hung up on him and called my cousin Kesha.

"Bitch, get up get dressed, FAST, I'm on my way to get you!" Click. Ten mins later.

"I'm outside!".

Kesha got in the car rubbing her eyes like she had just woke up, however she was fully dressed.

She asked me through a yawn "What the fuck is going on?"

"Bitch, remember that lie Teff told me about his baby momma? Well, he still sticking to that story after I saw them together, now his homeboy just told me to come to the room to do his hair and called back and said not to come because she there!"

"Oh, so we might gotta beat this bitch ass?"

"Right!"

"Not a problem."

My cousin was a ride or die for real and she loved her cousin, so it was multiplied. I chained smoked cigarettes on the way over. I was so nervous. I had no plan. I just knew that I wanted to catch him with her to prove that he was the biggest liar in America. Did I want to fight this chick? No, but if I had to, my cousin had my back. I pulled up slowly to the motel when I spotted Teff and Brad standing outside. I rolled down my window and gestured for Brad to get in the car. Brad looked at me like he had saw a ghost and didn't move. Teff smiled and walked toward the car.

"Get the fuck away from my car."

"What?", his face balled up.

"What? Where yo baby momma at, where Saleena at?," I screamed to the top of my lungs.

He paused and gave me this look like he would give a nigga he wanted to fight.

"Yeah, like I thought, Brad, you go get your hair done or what?"

"Yo, I ain't in this shit."

"So, you go pull up over here and try me like that?"

"Try you? Are you crazy? You must be muthafucking crazy."

"Yo I got yo crazy", He pulled out a gun.

"Nika, let's go", Kesha said in the calmest voice.

"Nah Fuck that," I jumped out of the car.

"Nika get yo ass away from here."

"I ain't going no damn where, how you go get mad at me because you got caught nigga, then you go pull out a gun? Shoot me muthafucker!"

By this time Kesha was screaming.

"Nika get yo crazy ass in the car!!!!"

I looked back at Teff to surprisingly see a smirk on his face.

"Yo, this girl is crazy yo", he said looking back at his friends."

I walked back to my car slammed the door and sped off. I was on fire. "How you go get mad and pull a gun out on a chick?"

My cousin was just shaking her head.

"That was crazy, yall crazy."

I continued smoking my cigarette.

Teff called me the next day. I don't even know why I answered. This time he came at me differently. He actually apologized and admitted that he told a lie. He explained that he and Saleena were basically broken up but living in the same house only because he had not found another place to stay yet. He claimed they did not even sleep in the same bed. He was also afraid that if he left, that Saleena may not let him see Miguel. I explained to him that I could not have anything to do with him while he still lived with her. He shocked me when he said that he understood. So that was that. Honestly, I was a little disappointed that it didn't work out but how could things go on now that the truth was out?

CHAPTER 4

YOUNG, DUMB, AND IN LOVE.
Mid-July 2002

I began to work at Salon Profile and it was beginning to grow on me. It was indeed different, but adventurous. The hood was always adventurous, and it was right in the heart of it. The salon was connected to the neighborhood corner store called Mickies. Everyone in the neighborhood passed our door to get there. It was fun just going to get cigarettes and soda. Mickie was the owner, and he was old, mad and crazy. I think he actually hated people. He was mean as hell and cursed everyone out. No one took him too seriously, but when they did, the arguments were hilarious. Between crack heads asking for 50 cent and the boosters selling anything from clothes to car parts, I was never bored. I managed to snag a few walk-ins the first week, it could only get better.

Meanwhile, Teff would call me periodically just to have casual conversations and we were now more like friends. His car had broken down, so I agreed to take him and Miguel to the chiropractor a few times, as friends. Since the truth was out now, I simply picked him up at his apartment. He professed his love to me every chance he got so one day I called his bluff. Teff had very unique rims on his car (hub caps). I told him if he was really done with her and wasn't afraid of her finding out about me, I wanted his stereo system and for him to put his hubcaps on my car. He did it with no hesitation. I still wasn't sold.

One day when I pulled up, Teff was about to fight the tow truck man. Every time the poor man tried to walk close to Teffs car, he pushed him halfway across the parking lot. He was furious. When he finally got in the car, he explained that the apartment complex was trying to tow it because it had broken down in someone else's assigned space. As I began to back the car up, I heard Teff say under his breath, "Ahhh shit." I looked in the direction he stared at through my back window to see Saleena walkng toward my car. I let out a long sigh. Let the drama begin.

"Stop the car for a minute," he jumped out, turned around, looked at me in my eyes and said very sternly, "Don't get out the car!"

I just looked at him, he looked back at Saleena then back at me,

"Ok boo?"

"OOOOOK!," I snapped back. I hung my arm out of the window, lit a cigarette, and watched them converse. She was clearly pissed. I wondered what he was saying to her, they were too far for me to hear. When he got back in the car, I didn't even look at him, nor did I say a word. There was complete silence to, during and back from the chiropractor. When we returned from the chiropractor, I politely told him, "You go have to find you another ride to the chiropractor from now on." He gave me the saddest look and mumbled "Aight" and walked in the house.

Hell, I was sad too, but I refused to continue dealing with some nigga AND his chick. I guess I'll see you next lifetime buddy.

He continued to call me, but I wasn't all that concerned about him. I had successfully made it through my first week at a shop and was well into my next week. I was so proud of myself. Teff had now began to call and badger me about where I worked. I guess I was making a little noise on his side of town, and he'd heard about it. I refused to give him any information on my whereabouts. With all the flyers I had put out, I was sure that he would eventually find me out. He let me know that he would indeed find me. I stood stern and I was just fine with him investigating to find me, giving him the address would be too easy for him.

The very next day as I finished up my client's hair, I looked up to see no one but yours truly walking through the door. Those damn flyers I thought. He was grinning from ear to ear. He didn't say a word. I fought to keep a straight face. He laid a small teddy bear, a folded-up piece of paper, and a single key on my station. He kissed me on my neck and walked out the shop without looking back. I watched him until he disappeared before I investigated what was on my station. I grabbed the paper and unfolded it.

You said if I moved you will be mine

So, here's your key

616 Archdale Dr.

Lexington Green Apartments

See you tonight, hopefully.

My entire body heated up on the inside. I could hear opera singers, ocean waves and wind chimes. I was in la-la land for the next 30 mins. I absolutely could not wait to get off. I braided faster than I had ever braided before that day.

"Aight Sonya I'm gone!"

I walked up the stairs to the door and attempted to use my key when I felt the door being pulled open. He grabbed my wrist, pulled me inside then up against him. He squeezed me like he had not seen me in years. It was one of the best hugs I had ever had.

"This is it". I looked around nodding my head in approval. It was super clean, probably because there wasn't a thing in it. He led me back to one of the rooms.

"This is my room, well OUR room."

There was a radio, a blanket, one lamp and two sofa pillows. No sofa.

"Nice baby, it's real nice,"

When I looked up at him, his smile was extra-large. I could tell he was so proud of himself and so was I. I had a little time before I had to pick Symone up from daycare. Exactly enough time to make love all over that floor. That floor would never be the same.

He rode with me to pick up Symone from daycare. I decided to stay over at his place, so I grabbed a few things from my place for the night. Then I grabbed more the next day. Then more the next day. That continued daily. Finally, the weekend was here and Saleena had agreed to let Teff keep Miguel for the weekend. I let him drive my car to get him while I was at work. When he returned to pick me up from the shop, I could tell from the look on his face he was pissed about something.

"What's wrong?"

"Man, that bitch trifling."

I just looked at him.

"Look at this shit!" he handed me the diaper bag. The bag smelled like spoiled milk. It had old milk and dirt all inside. There was nothing in it but a dirty bottle that I would not feed to a dog. I got in the back seat with Miguel to further examine. He had on a diaper that needed to be changed badly and a stained t-shirt. His fingernails and toenails were dirty, and his neck was sour. I was pissed. I looked up a Teff. Our facial expressions matched. All I could say is,

"Let's go to Wal-Mart."

I marched straight to the baby section like I meant business. I could not believe this bitch. Yes I was only 20 yrs. Old, and I was only 16 when I had Symone, but I knew better than this. Even if you did not have much, you could at least keep the baby clean! I was furious, and I was going to fix it. I knew that Teff didn't have any money, he spent it all on the apartment. All I had was my booth rent that I planned to save, but it didn't matter. I grabbed a bathtub, bottles, diapers, soap, lotion, a few outfits, formula and even a few toys. Oh, and a new diaper bag. I was determined not to use anything this broad had sent. The look on his face was priceless. He kept looking at me shaking his head in disbelief and adoration. He told me that he loved me and that I was going to be his wife.

"Boo, where you get this money from? Boo, is this your booth rent?"

I just smiled.

"Boo, you spent your booth rent on Miguel?"

I didn't answer.

Where the money came from was not important to me, I was not going to let this innocent baby suffer when I had the cash. It felt so good to get that baby home cleaned up. Miguel slept like a baby should and his daddy thanked the shit out of me. We were all happy.

The next day Teff wanted to take Miguel to see his mom. I agreed but I was not enthused. We stopped by his mom's house one time before and she did not even acknowledge my presence. I had made up in my mind that she was very rude, and I straight up did not want to go. He explained that I would meet his mother Shelia, his two younger brothers and his mother's husband Alvin. He also had 17-year-old brother, Chad was not home that day. When we pulled up, he jumped out of the car, said he would be right back. I unbuckled Miguel and grabbed his things. Before I could close the door, Teff and his mom were coming down the sidewalk toward me. They both were smiling, hard. Teff grabbed the baby and she grabbed me as if she hadn't seen me in years.

"Let me meet this wonderful woman that looked out for my grandbaby. Hi, I'm Shelia," she introduced herself as if she didn't treat me like shit the last time I saw her. I didn't know how to feel, but I was smiling.

"My son told me what you did, and I just want to say, I really appreciate what you did for my grandbaby. Welcome to the family, daughter in law."

I was totally confused. The shock on my face turned into the biggest smile that my face could handle. I assured her that it was not a problem and thanked her. She grabbed my hand and told me come and meet the rest of the family. We walked up stairs over a steep hill with her holding my hand high to make sure that I didn't fall because the heels I'd worn weren't equipped for climbing two sets of stairs. Everybody came outside like roaches. Apparently, this so-called hero story about me saving Miguel had been announced before my arrival and they were all incredibly pleased with my presence. I felt like a million bucks.

CHAPTER 5

LET THE DRAMA BEGIN.
Mid-July 2002

I was speechless, I just gazed at Teff and blushed as we all sat out on the porch. I met his two little brothers Marlon 10 and Jake 8. They were so cute. I met his stepdad Alvin briefly, he seemed to be preoccupied with something in the back yard. Teff made a run to the corner store to grab cigarettes, a bottle of Boones Farm wine for me a Milwaukee's best for Shelia an Icehouse for himself. I had ball chatting with Shelia until he returned. Things were going great until Shelia's phone rang. It was Saleena. She handed the phone to Teff. His face immediately balled up.

"What? You said I could keep him til Sunday. Don't come over here with that shit".

I didn't say a word I just studied his face trying to follow the conversation.

"Man, this bitch talking about she coming to get Miguel now."

"Why she trippin? She said you could keep him until tomo....". Shelia cut me off saying,

"Now she calling again, here you answer it, you his wife," then shoves the phone in my face.

"He-llo."

"Who the fuck is this?"

I knew I had something to prove because all eyes were on me. Inside I was freaking out. Why would his MOTHER be so messy and hand me the phone? His wife? I was barley his girlfriend.

"This Nika, what's up?"

"Oh, hell no! He go put that ball headed bitch on the phone!" Click.

My heart was beating so fast. What was happening? Was she going to come over here? This was too much, I was ready to go, but it was clear we were not leaving. Shelia and Teff had begun to talk big shit. Shelia made it clear that if Saleena showed up at her house that she was going to cut her. Teff said that he was going to shoot her. I didn't say a word. I was just in shock as to how the evening took such an ugly turn. These people were crazy, and I could tell that they meant every word they said. That was the scariest part. About 15 minutes after the last phone call, a car drove passed the house.

"There she go!" Everybody stood up, except for me of course. I guess I didn't know the routine, because it seemed that everyone knew what to do but me. Teff took off running toward the back of the house. Shelia handed me the baby.

"Here, hold your son".

I caught Miguel because she basically threw him at me then proceeded to spit a blade out of her mouth into her hand.

"I'll cut that Bitch if she come over here with that bullshit!"

I was done. How? How does one laugh and talk and smoke cigarettes and drink beer then spit out an entire blade? This crazy woman had a blade in her mouth all this time. Why? I could not fathom this level of crazy at this moment.

Next thing you know Alvin and Teff come from the back of the house wrestling over a shot gun. I tried to hide the shock on my face. Was he really going to shoot her? Well, he did pull a gun out on me that one time so, ok yes, he was going to shoot this bitch. I never wanted to go home this bad in my life. I looked down the hill to see Saleena and her fat ass friend pulling up in front of the house. Next, I see Shelia slapping and yelling at Teff, and yelling at me at the same time. She told me to take my pretty ass in the house. I was happy to follow her directions because this was just a hot fucking mess. I laid Miguel down so I could peek out of the window and smoke a cigarette. I saw Teff and Shelia walking down the hill toward her car. Thank God Alvin had wrestled that shot gun away from Teff. However, he was standing at the top of the hill with it across his shoulder like a guard. I watched Shelia swing her head back and forth and point her finger all in Saleena's face. Teff kept walking up close, and Shelia kept pushing him back. His brothers were in the yard speculating, then all of sudden I saw them running up the hill toward the house. They both burst through the front door out of breath saying,

"She said she want the bald-headed bitch".

Then the other one says,

"Yeah, she wanna fight you".

Before I could say anything, Jake looked me up and down and said;

"You can't fight in that".

This prompted me to look down at myself and realize I had on a mini skirt and wedged heels. I guess I didn't think I'd need my fighting attire today.

Before I could look up, Jake handed me a pair of sneakers.

Nika J.

"Put these on."

The other brother quickly unscrewed the broom and handed me the stick.

"Here, beat her ass, we don't like her anyway."

What kinda shit is this?, I thought. I took a deep breath. I was on the spot and there was nothing I could do but take my bald-headed ass down the hill. I felt like this was my initiation into this crazy ass family. I wanted them to like me. I didn't want to lose Shelia's respect that I had just gained only hours ago however, I did not feel like fighting. I would have never come over if I knew it was going to turn into all of this. Everyone watched me prance down this hill like a model with a broomstick in my hand. I bet I looked like I meant business, and I did plan to handle it, but I was shaking on the inside. This girl was as ghetto as they come, and she hated me. In her eyes, I'd stole her man. She was going to kill me the first chance she had. This was the chance!

"You said you wanted the bald-headed bitch?", I asked like a bad ass.

Saleena attempted to step forward, but Shelia grabbed her.

"You ain't go touch her bitch!"

Whoop! Whoop! Guess who came to visit? The Police. I was saved by Shelia and the police. All the yelling turned into complete silence in a split second.

"What seems to be the problem?" Everyone tried to explain at once. Teff surprised me at how he knew how to clean up his act and talk to authority as if he wasn't acting a plum fool just seconds before. He told the officer the issue at hand. I was so nervous. I thought that he would for sure take Miguel and give him back to Saleena. To my surprise he explained that according to the law, he could not take the baby from one parent and give it to another. He said that they both had equal rights to Miguel until they took it to court and filed custody papers. Teff asked a lot of questions and wrote down all the information. Saleena just looked stupid and defeated, then finally took her defeated ass on home, without Miguel.

Monday morning as soon at the courts opened, we were downtown filling papers. Saleena was calling my phone like she was crazy. She talked cold cash shit on my voicemail, and I saved every message. I'd never been through anything like this, but I could tell that it was going to be a mess. Teff asked millions of questions. We talked on the way home about what they had told us. Basically, we had to prove that she was unfit. Not a problem. We also needed to prove that Teff could provide a better home than she. Of course, that started with proof of income.

I knew Teff sold drugs. I couldn't prove it, but one plus one equals two. However, I knew he wasn't good at it because he never had a lot of money. He would put a little gas in the car here and there. He would even go in family dollar and steal what we needed for the house. He stole movies for us to watch, even diapers for Miguel. I actually thought it was funny. It was adventurous. I never knew anyone who wasn't afraid to steal. I was raised to never steal. I bought all of the food we ate with my food stamps. I worked but I wasn't bringing in a lot because I had just started, and I had to pay my booth rent which was half of my money most of the time. I never wanted to question him about his money. I didn't want to embarrass him, and I could tell he was trying his best. Plus, we didn't need much. As long as our babies were happy, we had each other, and some weed, we were just fine. We were in love, and happy, and that was free.

Teff hung out in the motel during the day while I was at the shop. Every night he was at home with the kids and I. One evening he told me he needed to run out for a minute. When he came back, he put something in the freezer and sat down beside me. He said he had something to tell me. I was thinking, oh God what is it now? He stared into my eyes for a long time. He was so dramatic.

"I sell drugs".

I started laughing. "No shit Teff."

He was smiling and shaking his head.

"Listen, I sell crack cocaine." He got up and walked in the kitchen grabbed what looked like a ball of aluminum foil from the freezer peeled off the foil and laid it on the table.

"This a eight ball."

Wow. I was so excited. I'd never saw cocaine in real life. For some reason I expected it to look different than what it did. I reached out to touch it he grabbed my hand like I was a child. He told me that I was to never touch it. He said that it would go through my pores, and I could get addicted. He made me promise to never touch it. I promised. Then he pulled out a box of sandwich bags and a razor. He began to chop it into little pieces. He explained that these were dime pieces and cost $10. He dropped each piece in the corners of the bag and tied it into a knot and cut it. I thought they were so cute. He did that until he had a bag full of little bags. He explained that he had paid $125 for it and when he sells them all, he will make $300. I thought that was pretty cool. He kept it inside an empty box of fish sticks inside the freezer. I felt so gangster for knowing how to sell drugs.

Now that the secret was out, he would openly chop his work into all dimes on the coffee table when the kids were away. I loved to watch. I wanted to help. It looked like fun. Maybe if I helped, we would have more money.

We were always broke. He never asked me for any bill money, however taking care of Symone, Miguel, booth rent, and gas was enough. While we waited for a court date, Teff and I played house. Over a short period of time, I had basically moved half the contents of my apartment into his apartment. It just made sense because I already had everything. Neither of us could afford to buy all we needed at his house. I was doing ok, but not excellent. I was still building my clientele. I was able to survive because my dad was having issues with my mom, so he just stayed at my place and was now paying the bills there. Teff's apartment was three mins from the shop and two minutes from the motel, it was so much easier to stay with Teff. We wanted to be together all the time and he had nothing. So, when it was time to shower, there were no towels. When it was time to cook, no dishes, no pots, no microwave. Now it's time to clean, no vacuum, no broom. Ok let's watch a movie, wait there's no t.v., vcr or videos. Teff randomly had a pull-out couch in the living room one day when I got in from the shop. No sheets. Symone needed toys. I had an extra daybed and Symone's old crib for Miguel. Before we knew it, we lived together.

Everyone was happy. While I was at the shop Teff would wash the clothes and run our errands. I would let him take my car and my phone like it was ours. Everything was ours; we did EVERYTHING together. We even took every shower together every day. We were in love. We even switched kids to learn to care for them both. He was such a wonderful father. Each night he would feed Symone and read her a book after her bath. At the same time, I would bathe Miguel feed him and put him to sleep. Then we would take our shower together, smoke a blunt and make love, recklessly unprotected. It was beautiful.

I had been so busy with Teff, I hadn't seen Chi Chi in what seemed like ages. Ok, 5 days. She told me that she had major things to tell me and needed to come over. Chi Chi's talks were always juicy, so I was super excited. Teff didn't like anyone around me other than his family, my father and Chi Chi. He was very protective. It didn't bother me much, but I noticed it. Even though I had met the guys at the room, once I had become his girl, I never saw them again. Even Fred, his best friend acted as if he was terrified of me. I thought he was so weird. If he had come by and Teff wasn't home, he'd act almost as a slave, Teff being "Massa" and I being his perfect white wife ready to tell a lie on him. He would give me no eye contact and damn near looked at the floor if I was in the room. Maybe, it was just a respect thing. Anyhow on this particular day, Chi Chi walked in talking on the phone with someone. She was using her white girl voice, so I knew that it was serious. Luckily, Teff was busy talking to Fred so we dipped off into the back room. Otherwise, he would have been back there with us. I sat beside her and tried to read the conversation through her face, but the things she said were too farfetched to follow. I held my breath for the explanation which began like this;

"So, you remember when I told you how I didn't want to work but I wanted a lot of money right?"

I stared at her like what the fuck.

"I started working for an escort service."

"Man shut the fuck up Chi Chi".

"No, listen, so I'm supposed to go out on dates with these rich ass old men".

"You fucking old men Chi Chi?" I yelled in disgust.

"Hell no, at the end of the date they pay me, I'm supposed to go fuck em, but after I get the money, I go to the bathroom then I dip".

I laughed hysterically, "That's my girl!"

"Now I'm fired".

"Damn right you fired, them crackas mad too".

"Hell yeah."

We both laughed.

"But I got another lick though". We just stared at each other with sneaky grins.

"Tell me".

"I gotta show you, I need you to ride with me real quick and Imma give you $100".

"What Imma tell Teff though?."

"I got it".

"Bet".

We both walked into the kitchen while Fred and Teff were conversing about some nigga shit and joined in on the puff puff pass as if we had been there all along. I just fell back to watch her do her magic. Teff was in charge, if you weren't in good with him, you couldn't get anywhere near me. However, Chi Chi always had a way to get passed all the rules. She joined in the conversation and then quite smoothly asked him could I ride with her somewhere really quick. His entire face changed, and the room turned deathly silent as if the D.J. cut the music off in the middle of a party. I held my breath.

"For what?"

"It's only go be like 30 minutes......."

Blank stare.

"She go come back with $100".

"Why yall still here?" He and Fred laughed exchanging the last of the blunt.

"Boo, bring back another cigar", he asked while bending over to give me a kiss and a shot gun.

Bingo, we got the hell out of dodge before his high ass even thought about it too long and he started asking a million questions as he loves to do.

Doing anything with Chi Chi was always an adventure. Besides the fact that I just adored her, she was one of my favorite people to be around other than my dad of course. We just understood each other. I'd known her since I was 12. I'd met her in 7th grade over an argument over Allen Iverson and we'd been inseparable ever since. We were next door neighbors for years and did all of our dirt together. All of the trouble I had gotten into during my teenage years involved her. We had even birthed our daughters together on the same day a few hours apart. She was the sister I'd never had. The bottom line was, we did not need to be together for we were, Pinky and the brain, Ren and Stimpy, Bonnie and Clide and Beavis and Butthead combined. Here goes more trouble.

I was so eager to know what this crazy girl had schemed up for this quick cash. I just hoped we wouldn't get killed or locked up. I wasn't too worried because although devious, Chi Chi was EXTREMLY Smart. Too smart for her own good.

Before we could exit the neighborhood, she proceeded to make a phone call. I watched her push a million buttons, so I knew this phone call was not a normal one. Then, she turns on her white girl voice.

"Hi guys I'm Linsey, I'm looking for guys in the Charlotte area looking for some fun adult entertainment! Can't wait to connect."

I'm looking at her like what the fuck is she doing. Within seconds she continued,

"Hi, send me your number".

She hangs up. I saw her push *67 to block the number before she dialed again.

"Hi, Chuck, you wanna hook up right now? Well first let me ask, are you the cops?If you're the cops, you have to tell me or its entrapment".

She puts the call on speaker for me to hear this nervous man stuttering insuring her that he is indeed not the cops and her insuring him that she wasn't either. Once the legalities were cleared up Chi Chi proceeded to give him three to four descriptions of women along with names off the top of her head. She did it so well I was wondering, were these chicks real? He chooses one of the descriptions.

Then she explains, "Ok sir, this is what is going to happen. The fee is $300 for an hours' worth of service. The house mom will meet you. You are to pay her and show your identification for security purposes. We MUST keep our ladies safe. After you pay the house mom, she will direct you to the hotel where you can start your service. After your service if everything goes well, you will be provided with a business card so you can then contact us directly. Does that sound good hun? Ok let's meet, say at the McDonalds on Tyvola.....ok hun see you in a few!"

"Biiiiiitch!!!!!"

"Girl, these white men are so dumb."

But I know you don't really have a chick in this room."

"Nope, and it don't matter, that's why I get the money first, by the time he realizes he done got got, we gone. And we can't get in trouble. What he go do? Call the police and say, "Yes officer I tried to buy some pussy and the pussy wasn't there?"

"Riiiight" I said, laughing hysterically! We both continued to laugh until a car pulled in and parked.

"Wait, I think that's him, he said he's in a blue car."

This weird, terrified looking white guy creeps across the parking lot toward our car.

"Hey Chuck, let's see your I.D."

She hands it to me. I pretended to copy down the information because the pen she handed me did not really work.

"And your payment."

She quickly stuffed the $300 bucks in her bra.

"Ok Chuck you see the Hilton across the street? Megan is over there waiting in room 3367. Ok, have fun!"

She handed me a $100 bill as we pulled off.

"Oh my God that was toooo easy."

We shared a mutual sneaky grin.We walked back in the apartment super hyped and told Fred and Teff about our lick. They were quite impressed. We got even more lifted to celebrate the victory.

CHAPTER 6

WAIT, THERE IS MORE.
Early-August 2002

Most of my money came from walk ins. The few clients I did have, were from the other side of town where my apartment was. I was the new chick in town over in this hood. Periodically, dudes would peek their head in the shop just to get a look at me. I was flattered, but I needed the money, not compliments. I spent a lot of my time smoking cigarettes in front of the shop and getting snacks from Mickies. I couldn't get enough of that store. Mickie would see me daily and never speak, he just stared at me like he didn't want me in the store. I would go in the store a few times a day and he would just look at me like I ran over his dog. The store was run down and smelled funny. He seemed to hate his life, wife and everyone that came near him. I was high most of the time, so I thought it was funny to speak to him loudly just to piss him off. One day when I was outside smoking, some guy with a large afro leaving the store asked me to braid his hair. Hell yeah! A new client was just what I needed because I had not made a penny the entire day. After I finished my cigarette, we walked in together. We had a short conversation about how he wanted his hair, then to work I went. With most of my client's male or female I carry on conversation. It would be really awkward for it to be silent for thirty mins to an hour. Besides, I was a talkative person, I entertained with my words. It made the time pass quickly and it didn't seem much like work. I like to think I'm a little funny, obviously this guy did as well. It was just my luck that yours truly decided to grace us with his presence just at the peak of our laughter.

"Can I holla at you for a min?"

I quickly looked up startled by his voice and a little confused might I add. I asked my client if he would excuse me for a moment. Teff held the door open for me then directed me away from the glass door.

"Why you up in here he-heing and ha-haaing with that nigga?"

I just looked at him for a long time before I asked,

"What?"

"Yeah, you in there having a good old time ain't you?"

"You crazy," I began to walk back towards the shop door.

"Oh I'm crazy?", He handed me my keys to my car and my phone and walked off.

I flipped him off as I entered the shop. Sonya walked out of her area.

"Nika, everything ok?"

"No, he think I'm messing with this dude," Sonya shook her head.

"See, he messing with yo money."

"Yo, that's your boyfriend?", my client asked.

"Yeah" I answered rather embarrassed.

"Yo, I heard that nigga crazy."

"He just stupid" I replied.

I finished braiding him up and smoked a couple cigarettes to calm my nerves and wrap my mind around what had just happened. I was reluctant to hurry home, so I decided to waste some time.

"Sonya, you got some bleach?"

I didn't even know how to mix it because I had never used it. Sonya coached me through the process. I stared at myself and the white creamy substance that covered my head as I continued to think about what had happened earlier. It was confusing to me that he was so upset for no reason, nothing had even happened. It was all in his head. Why would I cheat? I was happy, I lived in worked on his territory which was like a foreign country to me. Besides, he had my car AND my phone ALL day. What could I even get away with anyway?

My hair turned out beautiful. I decided to cover it in a doo-rag so it could be a surprise. Maybe if I looked extra beautiful, it would somehow calm him down or at least detract him. That is if me coming home extra late didn't make it worse.

My heart was beating so fast as I walked up the stairs. I did not feel like arguing, especially about nothing. He was so upset. Hell, he had walked all the way home. That wasn't a short walk. By the time I got to the

top of the stairs, he opened the door then sat down.

"What's up", he asked.

"You tell me?" I just stared at him. This dude was really upset, but so was I. I raised my voice.

"Teff, I'm in the shop tryna make some money then here you come with that bullshit, I don't even know that muthafuka!"

"Oh, you don't?" he stood up and walked towards me aggressively.

"So, you didn't fuck that nigga?"

"What? I just met him TODAY! I don't even remember his name!"

"Look don't lie to me cause I already know the truth, if that's what you do that's what you do!"

I turned all the way around (being dramatic) ready to say something super bad ass but when I looked at him again, he looked like another person. He had this evil grin on his face like he had really caught me in a horrific lie.

"I told you I don't even know that muthatfucker" I stated again sternly but calmer than my first. I tried to read this look on his face that was making me a little nervous.

"Oh, you know him, and you a trick and I don't want no hoe for a wife."

"Hoe? What the fuck is wrong with you? You crazy!"

"You go stop calling me crazy like I can't see what the fuck is going on."

He started pacing back in forth.

I couldn't even hear what he was saying because I was too busy focusing on what he was doing and forecasting he what may do next. I watched him intensely as he threw pillows and punched them in the air.

One eye was watching him destroy the living room and the other was looking for my car keys.

Who in the hell is this dude? This was not Teff, it was like he was possessed.

My eyes remained glued to him. I was confused and scared. To hear a man who treated me like no less than a princess call me a hoe had me all messed me up. I had to get the fuck away from him. He turned his back, and my ass was halfway down the stairs.

"Where you think you going?"

"Fuck you, you crazy!!," I yelled in between breaths from my dramatic get away.

I jumped in my car and locked the door just seconds before he attempted to pull the door open.

"Open the door boo," he asked calmly and out of breath.

I turned the key in the ignition and shifted to reverse. He ran and stood behind my car.

This nigga go make me run his ass over I thought. My heart was racing. What is he going do? Should I kill him? Is he going to kill me? It would definitely be better for me to kill him first. I just stared at him through the rear-view mirror breathing heavily contemplating what would happen next if I didn't give blue eyes some gas. I took my eyes off of him for one second and he was at the driver's window.

"Boo I'm sorry, I didn't mean to scare you, I was trippin, open the door so we can talk."

I stared into his eyes. I could tell he had snapped out of the crazy person he had turned into just 10 mins ago. But was it a trick? What if I opened the door and he beat me to a pulp? I had been through this kind of shit before, and I refused to deal with this type of person again.

"Please boo, I'm sorry, let's just talk, please don't leave me". His voice changed and it seemed that his knees got weak as he said it, as if me leaving him would be too much to bare.

I do not know why I believed him. I turned off the ignition and just sat there, smoking. He continued.

"I love you, I don't want to lose you, just let me explain."

I reluctantly opened the door. The smile on his face screamed, thank you, and I'm sorry!

He grabbed my hand and pulled me close to him so quickly it scared me. He held me so tight. Our dumb asses walked back up the stairs together and back into the house.

"Don't leave me, I'm sorry I love you." I just looked at him. I was still super confused. His demeanor had totally changed as if he wasn't the maddest nigga in the world only minutes ago.

"I need to tell you some things, I've been through a lot, I don't trust anyone."

I looked at him for maybe an entire min before I said a word.

"I'm not tryna be funny, but whew, I need a drink."

We both busted out laughing and headed to the ABC store for vodka and the corner store for cigarettes and cigars. We sat in the middle of the living room floor like kids and prepared for what turned out to be one the craziest stories I would ever hear.

The first thing he told me was that he was born in Boston and had been in foster care since he was 4 years old. His mom was on unfit, and they took him from her. When I asked about his dad, he brushed it off as if he did not exist. He said that he stayed with so many people, some were good, some were bad. In school he had become an excellent swimmer and won a few medals. I could tell he was proud of that. However, in one of the foster homes he stayed in they didn't take care of him well, so he had to figure how to make some money to care for himself. Somehow, he got caught up delivering packages (drugs) for some big-time gangster. He figured that he could add some money on the top of the delivery price to make himself a better cut. He got away with it for a while, but he eventually got caught. He thought the dude was going kill him but instead he commended him for his cleverness and gave the name Teff, short for Teflon. I had no idea what Teflon was. He explained it was an extremely tough material that coated bullet proof vest. I thought that was dope. He finally explained that the tattoo on his neck that said "Da Fam" had nothing to do with his family but attached him to some Folks up north(GD). He continued to tell me that when he was released from foster care at 18, he was basically homeless and left to fend for himself in the streets. They gave him his birth certificate, $100 and a hug. One night while being harassed by the cops out of sheer anger he beat a police officer's ass and took his gun. When he was caught, of course he ended up in prison for two years. Upon his release, his probation stipulations required him to live with a family member. I was so shocked at the fact that just a little over a year ago, he was reunited with his mom since the age of 4! They seemed like the had a great relationship. He told me that he resented Shelia for raising his brother Chad and not him. He explained that Chad was her favorite because she loved Chad's dad and hated his. I could tell that really bothered him. He really held a grudge toward her but loved her because she was his mother. I felt that. He had managed to amaze me yet again, and also, gained even more sympathy for his dreadful life circumstances that he no control over. I just wanted to make it all better. I decided that night that I was going to try my best to love all of his pain away. We made nasty "I'm sorry" love all night, literally.

It was perfect that court was the next morning. *My period came that morning as well.* Amazing. However, I still put on the prettiest dress I could find so I could really outshine this bitch. The dress looked awesome with my new hair color, which he loved. I looked great but I was so nervous, not to mention sleep deprived. Teff and Shelia didn't make it any better. They made such a fuss over me. Saleena had threatened me so much they were concerned that she would harm me if she caught me alone. So, they guarded me like dogs. I couldn't even go to the bathroom alone. I should have felt safe, but it only made me chain smoke cigarettes. We rehearsed what we would say on the way to court. There was no way she could win.

I saw Saleena and her fat ass friend as soon as I entered the court room. She rolled her eyes at me repeatedly. The way Shelia looked at her was definitely a threat. It was so tense. Teff took the stand first. He swore on that bible and then preceded to lie like hell. He told the judge how he was a used car salesman, (not true, but had paperwork) had an apartment (had not paid the rent), a car (my car) and childcare for Miguel (some old lady that stayed around the corner from Shelia (had not paid her either)). He even mentioned that his fiancé (me) was a hair stylist and planned to help him along with his mom. This was true. I could tell the judge was very impressed. When the judge asked him about Saleena, he gave this bitch NO mercy. The sad part was that it was all true. He described to the judge about the condition Miguel was in on the first weekend we had him. Next, he went on to how he did not feel comfortable with his son being in the house with Saleena, her sister, Saleenas other son and the sisters 5 kids in a two-bedroom apartment where all they did was smoke weed. Lastly was the icing on the cake, adding that she did not have a job and how she had made a sport of repeatedly threating me. The judge was disgusted and allowed him to come off the stand. I was not prepared for what she did next. She called my ass to the stand. I was literally shaking. Not only had I never stepped foot in a court room before, Shelia, Teff and this crazy bitch stared me down all the way to the stand. She asked me about the threats and wanted to know if I could prove it. Of course. I called my voicemail and actually handed her the phone full of her talking cold cash shit. The look on the judges' face was priceless. At this point I do not even know why Saleena would even attempt to come to the stand, but she did. I damned near felt sorry for her the way the judge picked her apart. She admitted she had no job and stayed in this home with all those people. Then the last question ended it all.

"Do you think you could pass a drug test today?".

She didn't even need to answer, her face told it all.

"Temporary full custody granted to the father, supervised visits may follow after D.S.S. investigates both households". Gavel!

Teff, Shelia and I hugged one another as Saleena cried. My sensitive ass thought about how it would feel to lose my child on the way to the car. My feelings were torn. I did indeed hate her because of the way she harassed me and how bad of a mother she was to Miguel. However, I did take her man and her son, I definitely understood her passion. I was a mother, so that part of me touched by heart, until I arrived at my car. This bitch had keyed the whole drivers' side of my car, in the courthouse parking lot! I wanted to kill this bitch. Teff was livid. We tried to get her in trouble, however the camera that faced the side of my car she keyed was not working that day. Lucky me. Fuck this bitch. I will never feel sorry for her again!

CHAPTER 7

THAT DAMN 8 TRACKS.
Mid-August 2002

My life had changed drastically, very quickly. The single life I once knew was over, and all of my time was consumed by, the shop, the kids and yours truly, The Teflon Don and ALL that came with him. I definitely wasn't the party girl anymore. Not to mention the fact that Teff started fights everywhere we went. This was definitely a reason to chill all the way out with the clubbing. We never went anywhere anymore. All we did was smoke weed and drink white liquor on the floor in the living room with his friends. Which wasn't the worse thing. Sometimes Shelia didn't keep Miguel over the weekend. Although I always had a sitter for Symone, I couldn't go out without Teff, that wasn't even a question. However, this particular weekend, I had finally made some real money at the shop. For the first time I paid my booth rent and I still had about $200 left over. Which was a huge deal, so of course I wanted to go and celebrate. I just wanted to dance. I missed everything about my social life, the loud music, drinks, the attention, and my friends. However, the thought of confrontation drained me. When I came home that night, I was so excited telling him about my financial success and how I wanted to go celebrate. He suggested that we go to Mothers. Mothers was a bar around the corner from the house that could get pretty thick on certain nights. Teff called up Fred and Fred invited his friend I'd met one time before. They drank a few pitchers of beer and I a few drinks. We tried to dance a little, but there was no dance floor. I was having fun, but not the fun I knew I could have at 8 tracks. Teff began to mention 8tracks in every sentence. I wanted nothing more but to go. After about 3 drinks, I looked Teff dead in the eyes and said to him very seriously "I just want to dance til I sweat, that's it, no bullshit!!!" Smiling from ear to ear, he assured me that there would be no shit and promised that we'd just go for about an hour or so then we will go home and fuck each other's brains out.

We were off. Fred rode with us and I'd invited my cousin Tamika to meet me there to occupy Fred. We were having a ball and we were highly intoxicated. We danced, the sweat dripped and a crowd gathered around us, again. It was the best high. We took a small break because Teff had to go to the bathroom, and I wanted to go to the patio to smoke a cigarette. While walking off the floor, Teff told me that he had saw someone that he didn't like. I asked him who it was, and he would not tell me and said he'd be right back. I proceeded to the bathroom, then outside with Tamika and Fred. Five minutes had passed, I'd began to worry. We decided to spread out and look for Teff. Fred and I returned back to our meeting spot to report no findings of Teff when we heard gunshots. Fred pushed me down on the floor and told me to stay as he ran toward the entrance of the club where the shoots came from. People were screaming and running away from the door and toward me. I was scared, but I still attempted make my way toward the front cautiously. I ran into my cousin, she was hysterical.

She screamed "Nika, they shot Teff! I saw him on the porch, I was on my way to tell him you were looking for him and somebody started shooting. I got pushed back in the corner!

"Is he ok?!", I asked in tears, fighting to get to the front of the club.

"I don't know I couldn't see!"

I cannot explain how I felt. Maybe scared, angry, anxious, and some more shit. What if he was dead? I would die. I was scared, but it did not stop me from fighting through this crowd to find to my man. The first thing I saw was Teff with blood all over his shirt, swinging at everyone who tried to touch him. Then he fell. Fred began to drag him into the men's bathroom. Of course, followed. He proceeded to fight Fred.

"Look man I'm just trying see where the blood coming from cus!"

"Let's go to the hospital, Teff where are the keys?" I began to feel his pockets. No keys.

We all looked around as we headed toward to door asking had anyone seen any keys. I found them in the gravel in front of the club. I was crying like a baby. He was shot in the forearm. Not a major area, but there was entirely too much blood for me to stay the least bit calm. I suggested that we just call the ambulance. That idea was completely shot down. Fred drove my car like a lunatic down Wilkinson Blvd. I sat up on my knees turned toward Teff in the back seat crying, screaming and asking a million questions.

"Nika! shut up and turn around before you make me pass out!"

I didn't say another word until I saw the ambulance and the cops heading toward the club. We flagged them down then pulled over. I felt a little better now that he was getting some medical attention because there was blood all over my back seat. They began to question us about who had shot him. Teff threatened me with his eyes. Hell, I really didn't know anyway, but I can tell he did, but he told them that he didn't. I guess this was that thug shit. Never tell the cops, so you can handle it later yourself with no interference or records. I didn't like it. Why was it such a secret? Why wouldn't you tell me. Why did someone want to shoot you anyway, hell what the fuck even happened? This added frustration, and confusion to that list of emotions.

The hospital wait was indeed one of the most dramatic waits ever. I had never witnessed an event as such. My little life up until this point was a little edgy, but never to this magnitude. I felt like I was living in some gangster movie, and I was not sure whether to play the girlfriend that remained calm for her man or the dramatic one that had to be lifted off the floor. I called Shelia, whom I thought would really bring the drama, but she was surprisingly very calm. She arrived just as Teff went back for surgery. I explained to her what the doctor had told Fred and I which was that the bullet had actually went straight through his arm. The surgery was to attempt to repair his nerves and stop the bleeding. Shelia had somewhat of an attitude. As if she didn't have time for this drama as if she hadn't always come with it herself. I was confused. She left before the surgery was over.

It was 7 am and I had to be at the shop at 8 am. I just took Teff to work with me because I didn't want him by himself. It was quite embarrassing explaining to Sonya what happened. She just did her infamous "Umm" and shook her head. I could tell that she was disappointed in me for being with him. She knew too much. She watched as he drove my car around with my phone all day and caused problems with my clients. She didn't say much and was rather soft spoken, something like the type of mother I wish I had. She would utter periodically "Don't let that boy mess up your money". I could not even be mad at her; her delivery was never overbearing and everything she said was true. I deserved better, I knew better, I wanted better, but I was stuck. The moment I was fed up with the drama, I would come home to dinner cooked, a bubble bath in a house full of sweet music, kids clean in the bed, and blunt rolled followed by the best sex ever. I loved this guy because of the way he loved me. I never had to question it. It was a security that made me question everything else. So, I would make excuses; "It's not his fault, crazy stuff always happen to him." I felt sorry for him and his constant misfortunes. I was his hug after a difficult day, he needed me.

I couldn't wait to get off, I was exhausted. As soon I got Teff home and in the bed my dad called.

"It's my daddy".

"Don't answer".

"But I got to, he just go keep calling".

Phone stops ringing and begins ringing again.

"See".

"Hey daddy". Teff was swinging with his good arm, whispering loudly "Don't tell him shit".

I tried to pretend everything was normal. Too bad my daddy knows me like the back of his hand.

He could smell the lies through the phone.

"Hell, nah let me speak to Teff".

Why?!!!!

"What's up! "Teff attempted to act normal.

"What the hell going on over there?".

Teff told him everything. On the inside I screamed, "Nigga is your hand on the Bible? This is so bad."

Then he asked to speak back to me. Great.

"Nika, what the fuck this nigga doing?"

"I don't know daddy" I could feel his aggravation with me about my decisions through the long pause before the call ended. What in the fuck am I doing?

As the days went by, Teff had gotten better and almost back to his old self. He finally ran out of the little bit of pain medication he had because he had no insurance, so I wasn't afraid to let him drive anymore. However, I had begun to feel some type of way about him having my car all day and coming back broke. I mean what the fuck was he doing all day? It did not help that Sonya had begun to question me about it.

"Yawl young girls, I tell you".

It was embarrassing. All week I tried to get up the guts to tell him that, I simply wanted my car back. Seemed simple huh? I knew that it would not be. I mean why couldn't I just leave the shop when I was done and drop Symone off alone? I wanted to ride in my car and drop off my child in my car alone. I wanted to roll the windows down and bump my favorite song, smoke a blunt and drive with my knee in peace slowly down 77. Even swing by a friend's house for a quick visit, alone, like it used to be. Teff NEVER LEFT ME ALONE. This could not be normal. Chi Chi wanted me to come hang out with her so we could shoot the shit like we used to. What was wrong with that? Nothing. But everything was wrong about it to Teff.

Fuck this. I wanted to go out tonight. I would tell him when he came to pick me up.

"Hey baby, listen, Imma drop you off at the crib and then I wanted to go chill with Chi Chi".

He looked at me like I said "I'm gonna fuck another nigga tonight." I promise that what he had to hear.

"Oh Yeah?" He asked before he jumped out of the car.

"You ain't gotta take me know where!"

I wanted to call somebody on his ass. I wanted my daddy to pull up, hop out of the car and beat his ass! I wanted to call up one of my hommies that I do not get to kick it with anymore to come show him what could happen when you fuck with me. But I couldn't. This motherfucker was crazy, I thought as I watched his dramatic ass walk back and forth like the crazy person he was. My daddy would have to shoot his ass, then he would go to prison, again. There's nothing you could do to get me to contribute to that. As far as my hommies, I wouldn't even want to introduce them to this magnitude of drama. Now what was I supposed to do? I had Symone with me and needed to drop her off. I called Chi Chi and told her what was going on. She insisted on calling her baby daddy, Fat Man, I insisted that she did not. Fat Man was a helleva nigga but Teff was on some other shit. If Teff had gotten a fif of me calling in for help, he'd really flip. I just sat in the car waiting on Fat Man, nervous as hell chain smoking cigarettes. Teff had disappeared for a while leaving me with assumption he was gone. I had taken Symone into the salon and was standing in front of the salon door when I saw Teff reappear. He quickly opened my car door and popped my truck and my hood. At the same time Fat Man pulled up. I made it over to Fat Man as quick I as I could so I could explain the situation better than Chi Chi had. I could tell he was in defensive mode; I was like a sister to him.

"Look at me" I began to whisper and talk through my teeth demanding his complete eye contact. "I just want you to take Symone to Chi Chi, don't look at him, don't say shit to him, he crazy."

"Nigga Girl you need me to handle this nigga?"

"Noooo....!"

We both looked over at Teff because he slammed the trunk closed. He grabbed a machete out my trunk and headed toward my hood.

"Teff get away from my car!" Of course, he did not listen. I ran in the salon to tell Sonya and grab Symone. Sonya followed me out of the shop. I proceeded to get Symone in the car with Fat Man. At this point the situation had drawn a small crowd.

'Young Man! Young Man! Leave that girl car alone!"

"I ain't doing nothing to her car", he slammed the hood closed and put the machete back in the trunk. Then he walked over to the fence beside the salon and punched it.

"Don't come back up here no more!" she yelled at him as she walked back into the salon.

I didn't want to say anything to Fat Man but he was of course interrogating me at this point. I assured him that I would fine and all I needed was for him to drop Symone off for me. Finally, he left then Teff left, well at least I thought. I leaned against the brick wall inhaling my cigarette slowly trying digest this bullshit and preparing for the rest of it because, it was not over. I knew, it had just begun. I basically lived with this man, I had to go there tonight. The only other option was to not go home and piss him off even further. A few people from the crowd we drew asked if I was okay. How embarrassing. If I went inside the salon, Sonya would definitely lecture me and I was NOT ready to go home yet. I walked over to Mickies and got a wine cooler the smoked another cigarette before I went inside.

"He can't come back up here no mo! That boy is messing up yo business. Ain't nobody go wanna get they hair braided if yo boyfriend up her causing all kinda drama."

"Yes ma'am."

I knew this was some bullshit. I knew the way he was was not right. Now he had shown everyone. Now I looked crazy too. No one understood. I loved him so much. No one knew how we took all our showers together. No one knew how well he treated Symone and how much of a great father he was. No one knew how it felt when we made love. No one knew the things he opened up and trusted me with and the obligation I had to him to be different than everyone else who had betrayed him. I couldn't be like everyone else. I had decided to be that ride or die, I couldn't renege. I had to love him through this because he could not help it, he just loved me so much that it made him crazy. The truth was, I was secretly afraid to leave him. I was not sure what he would do if I did but I knew it wouldn't be good. If no one else knew, I knew, all he needed was to know someone loved him no matter what. That was who I was trying to be for him, now he goes and does this. Now I could not even take up for him because he let everyone see his crazy.

Frustrated and scared I drove around a little and finished my blunt before I headed home. My anxiety was through the roof. I was bad enough that I rode around with a machete because of Saleena, now I had go face this terrorist. I did not know what to expect. I thought about last time he flipped. Would this one be better, or worse?

I reluctantly walked up the stairs to our apartment. I heard music as I unlocked the door. It was pitch black dark inside and the music was loud. I felt around for the light switches, but none of them produced any light. Suddenly Teff appeared plugging up a lamp. I was shook. Why would he make the house dark like this? It was simply weird.

"So, where you been? I thought you were going out with Chi Chi?"

"Why ain't none of the lights working Teff, turn the music down!" I was scared, but also annoyed.

He turned the music down.

"Teff, you go have to chill, Imma have to do things without you sometimes and you can't act like this!"

"You ain't go be out here acting like a hoe".

"This yo last time calling me a hoe because I can take my hoe ass home."

"Bye, Bye Hoe"!

"Bet."

I didn't hesitate to walk out that door. Before my feet I hit the 3rd step, I was up in the air.

"Where the fuck you think you going?"

Teff had tossed me across his shoulder and carried my ass right back up the stairs and back in the house. I was terrified. What was he gonna do to me? I just prayed. Surprising he sat me on the couch gently, then proceeded to curse me out for being a sneaky bitch as so he called it.

I did not say a word. I had never seen anything like it. He paced back and forth as he talked shit and randomly threw shit around the room. I plotted my escape again knowing it had to be better than the first one because if I didn't get away this time, he would just get madder.

I thought about the time I tried to break up with Nigga Boy (my ex), which ended with me calling the cops. How do I get myself into this type of shit? As I sat there again, praying that this fit would soon come to an end I see Teff fall to his knees. He turned to me, face full of tears.

"I'm sorry boo! I'm sooooo sorry. I know you go leave me this time. I know you go leave me, but I promise, I'm sorry boo!".

I didn't move, I just analyzed. It appeared that he had snapped out of whatever trance he was stuck in now reality had hit him. He was genuinely sorry. It was like he was not in control before, but now he was and had realized what he had done, but it was too late. He was losing it again but with sorrow, not anger like before. It broke my heart. I felt terrible for him, I could feel his pain. I did not know what his problem was, but he was not himself before, this guy crying was the love of my life, the one that treated me like a princess. He told me that when he was young, he used to be on these meds, and they mellowed him out. He explained that he did not do things like this when he had those meds.

Whatever those meds were, we needed them.

"Well let's get you back on those meds."

I walked up and wrapped my arms around his head. He wrapped his long arms around my waist. He apologized repeatedly.

"I'm not go leave you Teff."

CHAPTER 8

WHO THE HELL IS ALONZO?
Early-September 2002

So out of the clear blue sky Teff begins to talk about this guy named Alonzo. Apparently, he hung the moon, and it was really weird to say the least. Teff was not the type of guy to brag about another nigga. However, this Alonzo nigga must have been the ultimate gangster. He had "just got out" and was coming over soon to catch up. Whatever. Teff was so dramatic, I did not feed into it much. I just hoped that this Alonzo nigga could help him get some money and keep him busy, so I could have a break from his daily antics. I loved him so, but all of the drama that came with him was wearing me the fuck out.

Up until this point Fred was the only friend Teff really fooled with, but I hadn't heard from him in a few weeks. When I would ask "Where's Fred?" He'd flip and be like "I don't fucking know, why you worried about that nigga?"

Of course, I wanted to ask, why haven't you EVER mentioned this Alonzo dude before? It wasn't even worth it. I tried not question this dude at all. He suggested that I'd hook him up with my friend Chi Chi. Sure, it seemed simple. Chi Chi was so finicky, I wasn't sure how that would work out. To begin with, she would definitely want a full report and at this point I got nothing beyond Teffs dramatics.

Finally, the infamous Alonzo arrived. I was NOT impressed. Well at least not at my first glimpse.

I assessed the situation as he greeted Teff. Now he wasn't UGLY, but he was dressed really nice and smelled great. Alonzo was average height, pecan tan and somewhat thick, but not fat. He introduced himself with incredible manners and shook my hand. I continued my assessment. Nice gold chain Mr. "I just got out". Oh, and is that a Lexus key on the table sir? What the fuck is going on? I had sized him up in the first 20 seconds. I automatically assumed that he was some type of drug dealer. He surprisingly interrupted my judgement with one statement.

" Hey, so I didn't know what you drank so I just got some Grey Goose".

"You shouldn't have", I grabbed the bag out of his hand quicker than the word goose could leave his lips and hurried to the kitchen.

Teff watched me laughing and dapped up Alonzo explaining to him how much I loved Grey Goose. I quickly turned into a bartender then returned with three cups to the living room floor where Teff had sat up the chess board.

We smoked and played chess which was one of our normal day-to-day activities. About an hour later, Chi Chi finally arrived (she was always late).

I could tell that she did not like him from the look on her face. She gave a fake happy "Heeeeyyyy". This would be another issue I'd have to deal with later. I could hear Teff in my head already. "Why yo girl acting like that with my boy?" I don't fucking know or fucking care TEFF!!! But of course, I wouldn't say that. I picked my battles with him carefully. She lingered around for all of 20 mins before she made up a reason to leave. Typical Chi Chi, of course, she never showed up again but always said she would. This repeatedly left Alonzo as the third wheel at every visit. I can't say I minded his visits. I actually liked him a lot. He was super laid back. Teff and I never did much because he never had any money so Alonzo coming over started to be the highlight of the day. He never came empty handed. He would always bring, something to drink, smoke or eat. Who would have a problem with that? Everything was cool for a few weeks before things started to become little awkward.

See here's the thing. Teff's lack of finances wasn't a deal breaker for me because, I was actually in love. However, I had experienced life before Teff.

I guess because I never talked about it, Teff assumed either one, my life never existed before him, or two, it was worse or similar. This was far from the truth. The truth was, my life was far better before him.

Teff did not realize that although young and inexperienced I ran across a few that did have it. Money that is. You know that saying out of site out of mind? Well, that's what I can chalk things up to at this point. Teff had me completely out of my element. Therefore, I was not even around the things I'd been introduced to. At this point I was barley even around anyone but him and his family. I was on another side of town that was another world to me, and it belonged to him. Everyone in this area knew him and that I was his girl. No one would dare approach me because he was crazy, and they knew that I was his pride and joy. I had a permanent no trespassing sign on my back for everyone to see that he did not invite in.

Let me paint you a picture.

My apartment in a far better area on the other side of town was based on my income which was practically NOTHING due to my circumstances. I received a check for my daughter along with food stamps. I did hair in my house (no booth rent). I had plenty. Not to mention, I had the ability to attract most men but especially the ones that wanted to "give me the world". I had no one to answer to, no drama and not a care in the world. Now here I was, moving all of my shit into Teffs place, spending every dollar I made all in the name of love. Alonzo coming around reminded me of what I was missing. I couldn't even be myself. I was damn near afraid to talk to him. Everyone stayed away from me because of how Teff was about me, but not Alonzo. He was not afraid to just talk to me. He was never disrespectful, he just simply acknowledged my presence, and I loved that. Teff never seemed to mind.

Usually when Fred came over to play chess with Teff, the floor was not open for discussion. Besides Fred being afraid to even look at me, conversation wasn't even an option. During the game of chess I was forced to be quiet, or I was scolded by Teff, which was embarrassing. So, I just fettled around deathly bored, high with so much to say, wishing Chi Chi would answer the phone. Alonzo was different. He would actively engage me in conversation, asking me how I was doing and how was my day. I ate it up and struggled not to show it, afraid that Teff would kill me when he left.

Surprisingly, I didn't receive much feedback from Teff. Alonzo's visits slowed down a bit from the initial hype, but he was now like a part of the family. He would come over periodically and Teff and I eventually found ourselves at Alonzo's crib.

All I said was that I was hungry.

Alonzo pulled out a $20 bill and his keys and said to take his car to go get all of us all some food. I quickly looked at Teff to receive his reaction. He pretended as if it was no big deal, but I knew better.

I felt like a boss driving his big boy Lexus to McDonalds. I missed this feeling. I was alone, looking good in a nice car, windows rolled down, with the music bumping. I like this shit. I soaked it all in on the way there, but on the way back I thought. I thought about how the way I felt at that moment was where I wanted to be. I was never alone with my thoughts for long anymore. All of my thoughts were interrupted by HIS issues, or something connected to HIM. Then I had nothing, he had nothing. I missed being in the wind, calling my own shots, answering to no one. I missed attention and flirting. Hell, I missed being a hoe. I missed making my own money and spending it only on me and my baby. I remembered how I had plenty before I thoughtlessly took on all of this responsibility. I felt pulled down deep into a hole looking for a small light. There was no light, until today. I didn't even get to see but a split second of it, but I saw it as the sun set on the way to McDonalds. I wanted to see it again. I pulled back into the driveway realizing I had forgotten to do my real thinking on the drive back because I was so busy enjoying it. The real thinking was this. This Lexus was huge compared to Neon and I was high, as shit. Hell, I almost hit my own car pulling out but got the feel of it on the way out. Why would Alonzo let me drive is beautiful freshly waxed luxury vehicle? I suddenly had a flash back of all the perverted old men that just let me do all kind of unorthodoxed bullshit just for the bounce in my breast from my jump of excitement and to see the way the shiny lip gloss sparkled off of my braces. Oh, my gawd, did Alonzo want some pussy? Teff is going to kill him. I sat in the car deep in thought afraid to go inside. How do I unsexy myself? Wipe my lip gloss off? Not let my hips sway from side to side when I walk? That was too much work. I was too high to stay focused on all those changes. This thought interrupted all my thoughts. I had better get my ass inside before the fries had gotten cold and Teff would swear that I stopped by a whole other niggas house in a whole other niggas car, and fucked this nigga on the way to get my nigga some Mcdonalds. In his mind this could happen. I put on more lip gloss, and decided to walk slow, switching extra hard like I had just parked my Lexus. Then I stuffed fries in my mouth and refrained from any eye contact with anyone but the kids....

The ride home was quiet, but I enjoyed it. I turned Tweet up loud, hit the blunt, layed my seat back and propped my feet up on the dash while staring at the beautiful sky. Things had to get better.

I hated when I couldn't tell what he was thinking. I pretended as if there was not an elephant in the room. We put the kids to bed as usual.

My dad had cartons of cigarettes. It was better that I did not know why or how. All I knew is our broke asses needed some. He said he would come over later. Meanwhile Shelia had informed Teff that she was coming over too. She was having issues with Alvin, her husband. He was aggitted.Teff told me that we cannot smoke around her because she was a recovering addict. Addict? This was never mentioned before, why was suddenly a big deal. We can't smoke, what the hell else were we going to do? I have never seen her without a beer or cigarettes in her hand so what was the difference? Whatever. She came over acting rather strange. Or drunk. Or something else. She sat on the floor with us in the living room. I tried to make small talk like I wanted her over. It seemed that she planned to stay the night, but I wanted to fuck my man so I was super agitated. The subject was Boston Massachusetts, where they both were born when Teff went to the bathroom. As soon as the door closed Shelia got really close to me and began to whisper loudly. First, she made me promise to never tell Teff. Then she very quickly tells me that; Teffs dad was her pimp and that he got her addicted to heroin. She said that he would shoot it in her arm in her sleep, he got her addicted to control her. Then she added, that he did this even while she was pregnant, therefore Teff was born addicted. I must admit, I was still high and now a little drunk, so the severity of this information did not mean so much to me right then. I was just confused as to why she decided to tell me this shit now! Teff walked out the bathroom and we both sitting mad close looking stupid.

"What yall talking about?"

Luckily as soon as Shelia started to ramble a lie that I could tell she was going to screw up, my dad knocked on the door. He came in grinning.

"Who is this beautiful lady?"

Ahh damn. My dad was now a newly single man. Just recently, him and my mom had a huge falling out at some baseball game. I was on my dad's side so I would not have cared, but this was Teffs mom. We had enough drama. My dad was fresh out of an 8-year bid, he had not gotten his run out, trust me. Him flirting with Shelia was dad news. I tried to give him a look. He ignored me and proceeded to charm Shelia draws off, literally. Next thing I know my dad had volunteered to take her to the store to buy all of the things she said she did not have to spend the night with him, at my house, because that is where he stayed. I just smoked more weed and tried minding my business because these people are grown, I think. I just knew this would cause problems later. Either way, I was glad to get them out of the house so I could get nasty with Teff.

Afterwards he looked at me and said, "You pregnant".

I laughed "Why you say that?"

"My uncle said, if it feel real good when you pee after a nutt, you got somebody pregnant."

"Oh really? You want another baby?"

"I ain't go lie, that would be a lot right now, but you my wife, so we'd figure it out."

"You want a boy or girl?

"Girl".

"I want a boy"

"It don't matter, it'll be wit my boo."

"I love you Teff"

"Love you more boo"

CHAPTER 9

MORE FUEL FOR THE FIRE.
Mid-September 2002

It had been a few weeks since Teff had been shot. He had finally gained feeling back in his fingers and was using his arm a lot more. His arm being in a sling did not stop this motherfucker from being crazy. Saleena was still giving us problems. We had Miguel fair and square. The social worker had come out to inspect our apartment and we passed with flying colors. The courts had not even granted Saleena any visits yet. She hated us, especially me. Hell, I hated her ass too. She had keyed my beautiful indigo blue neon "Blue Eyes "and any given day I would come home to this bitch sitting in the parking lot. Now that we had Miguel, she refused to give us any of his things. Things that Teff claimed, he purchased (probably stolen) regardless, we needed it. She was being spiteful and part of me understood, but part of me was like, fuck that. Teff had the bright idea to break in and take it. I never understood why he did not have the key. Who knows. I had a fever and was in the bed (pull out couch) drinking soup, you know, being sick, when Teff suggested with a sense of great urgency that we go break into Saleena's apartment and at that very moment. Why Teff? Why now? I hopped my sick ass in the car looking like death wearing Teffs oversized clothes. He explained on the way there that she was at work, and we must do this now. He had a plan. He would open a window that he knew she kept unlocked and I would climb my tiny ass in and unlock the door. So, I did. I was nervous as hell, but I did not show it. I had never broken into anything before. Although we had knocked on the door to assure no one was there, I still had in the back of my mind, what if there was. I knew I would try to kill anyone coming through my window without a second thought, now here I am. The apartment was filthy. When Teff lifted me through the window, I landed in a sink full of nasty ass dishes. The house smelled like dirty diapers and some other shit I do not know how to describe. Teff took everything. I could not believe Miguel had so much stuff. I understood why he was so pressed to get his stuff. I sat in the car as he filled it up with Miguel's things. Just to be a bitch, I shoved my flyer in her door. Checkmate Bitch!

The next day I took the car to work because I only had one appointment and was determined not to sit another beautiful Saturday away waiting. I had harassed Shelia for the past few days to come and cook dinner at our house with a special request, macaroni, and cheese. For some reason I was craving it, but not just any macaroni and cheese, only Shelia's macaroni and cheese. She had finally given in and called and said she was on the way to the house. It was my lucky day. I called Teff to tell him to be at home to open the door for Shelia and the boys. I finished up my client, then headed home. I was so excited just to lay on the couch watch a movie I had seen 20 times and eat half a pan of the best macaroni and cheese I had ever tasted. I walked in the house and headed directly to kiss the cook. I didn't see Teff. The boys (Teffs little brothers) informed me that when he let them in, he was pissed about some shit he had gotten into with some nigga at the store, then he said he would be back. My heart sank, followed by total panic. Teff was so confrontational. I was always afraid that someone would kill him. Him being shot had my nerves even more tore up. I used Shelia's phone to call him on my phone.

"Come home now!"

"Aight".

He walked in with the drama all over his face. He was all sweaty, breathing hard with his fist balled up. The boys ran up to him asking what happened. Shelia walked out the kitchen with a large spoon in her hand, other on her hip. I continued to lay there, but I was all ears.

He explained that while he was out washing clothes, some dude had headphones on rapping aloud to a song talking shit, but was looking Teff dead in the eye. So of course, Teff asked him who the fuck he was talking to. The guy said, "Not to you, but if I was..." Teff hit him in the mouth. Dude said he would be back. Teff followed up with going to borrow A.B.'s gun. Now here he was, with the gun.

I didn't say shit. I was waiting on the macaroni and cheese to cool off. I didn't feel like dealing with Teff's drama today. This crazy shit was his daily norm, I had accepted the fact that I was a mob wife and I just wanted to hold the big pretty gun.

Shelia says, "Instead of fighting, you need to worry about yo pregnant girlfriend."

We both said "Who?"

"Look at her."

Everyone's eyes landed on me at once, I even looked at myself. My pants were unbuckled, and I was laying on the couch letting that hot mac and cheese burn my mouth because I couldn't wait for it to cool off. Damn, was I pregnant? Look at me. Let's add the fact that all of a sudden, I could not find my birth control pills. It had been a while since I had taken it last, and we were anything but careful.

"I told you. Aww boo you pregnant?" he said touching my belly.

I smiled from ear to ear. "I don't know?" He kissed me a few times then let me hold the gun. I had never held a gun. I was shocked at how heavy it was. I thought it was beautiful now I was infatuated with it.

We later found out that the dude that Teff was beefing with, actually lived across the parking lot and a little down from us. There was tension all day. They sat on their porch, and we sat on our patio literally yelling back and forth talking shit to each other for hours. At one point, one of the guys (it was like 3 of them) pulled his gun out and shot up in the air.

Teff yelled "You can't kill the sky nigga!" We laughed along with his mom. We did not take any of this shit seriously until the cops pulled up. Teff was so good with cops. I watched from the patio as he charmed the cops into thinking he was the innocent one. The cops made them both agree in front of them that the beef was squashed. As soon as the cops left, Teff called his cousin Tony, his brother Chad, and a few other guys I did not know. They all showed up in all black like they planned it, but I never heard that detail when he called them, it was crazy. They stood in a circle in the middle of the street and chatted a little. Shelia the boys and I all watched from the patio. It had gotten dark.

The guys seemed to have assembled some sort of formation similar to a diamond with Teff in the front like the point. They walked straight down to that guy's house. I was nervous. They never ran the plan by me, what exactly they were going to do? Shelia told me not to worry and that they were just going to set things straight. Whatever that meant. I thought they had already done that when the cops made them squash it. I guess I was the only one that did not know what the fuck was going on.

They had arrived at the dude's porch. I held my breath. They were too far for us to hear what was being said but Teff was doing all the talking. Next thing I knew they were headed back, back turned, not looking back.

They all came in praising Teff. One of the guys bragged about how Teff walked straight up to the dude and said;

"I know you told the cops that the beef was squashed earlier, I don't believe you.

So Imma just tell you this; if anything happens to my house, my car, my girl or my kids; Imma kill you, yo mom and yo kids. Then he turned his back and walked all the way home without looking back. His brothers thought he was superman. I ain't go lie, that was cold blooded, but now what? My anxiety rose as everyone left.

I eventually fell asleep. I woke up in the middle of the night to find Teff still awake. He told me that he will not be sleeping because he needed to protect his family. Protect? This was out of hand. When I woke up the next morning, he informed me that he needed to keep the gun. He was very upset because he found out that A.B. told the guy he was beefing with that Teff had his gun, and that he had to give it back the next day. He felt betrayed. He felt like A.B. was trying to set him up. Was A.B. trying to get him killed? So, he really needed to keep this gun. He already had a plan, which of course involved me. I was to call A.B. and tell him that Teff had been locked up with the gun. He bought it. I was a great actress. I had even went as far as asking him to give me money to help get him out. Now we had a gun, but now Teff could not leave the house because if someone saw him, it would mess up our lie. Teff did not sleep for at least 3 days. I did not even think that was even possible. It is.

It had been a few days and Teff had finally fell asleep so I could bring Chi Chi up to speed. She cursed my ass out. She told me that I was stupid and that I needed to get the fuck out of there and that if something happened to her niece (Symone) that she would personally kick my ass. I knew that I needed to leave, but for some reason I couldn't. I was stuck. I knew that I was in danger. I knew that if I was, so was my daughter. What was I supposed to do? Leave? I needed him to do something personal to me to piss me off for me to leave. I was very unhappy, I was afraid, but I still could not leave.

CHAPTER 10

A LITTLE BIRDIE TOLD ME.
Early October 2002

I had convinced Teff that we needed to go to church. He agreed. At this point, I was so unhappy he would do almost anything to keep me from leaving. The service was wonderful. Tom F. Lee was an awesome gospel singer that I grew up listening to. He taught in a way I could understand. Unlike most services, I left with something. I did not talk to God as much as I should have, but now, I really wanted to.

Stopping by my cousin's house after church was like a ritual (when I went), so we did just that. I desperately needed to see Bug. Bug was Kesha's mom. She was a little older than my mom and I had lived with her before I had gotten my own place. She was like a mom; she was everything I wanted my mom to be. Kesha took it so lightly in my opinion. I probably felt like that because having someone like her at your disposal was her norm and not mine. Teff tried to come in, but I insisted that he stayed in the car and that I would not be long. The truth was, I wanted to talk to her about him and have some privacy, for once. I had zero privacy. I was so heavy, with nowhere to unload. My mom and I were not on good terms which was beginning to seem like our norm, but I was in terrible need of a MOMMY! She asked me what was wrong on site. I asked her why she asked me that. She told me that I looked tired, drained, and stressed. Damn, I thought I carried it well. Well maybe well enough for a few, but not for Bug.

I explained that I was very unhappy and why, which consisted of all things dealing with Teff.

She asked me one simple question.

"Why don't you just leave?"

It seemed so easy, the way she put it.

"I kinda feel sorry for him Bug, he not go make it without me, he needs m...."

She cut me off and raised her voice just a little.

"Don't you ever feel sorry for no man, a man is a man. Now if you not happy, LEAVE! Go get happy!"

I didn't say a word. I just stared at her nodding my head yes. I felt like I was in a locker room just seconds before a big game. This was my pep talk. I was ready to score. I think.

I managed to utter, "Yes ma'am" as one tear fell.

Bug quickly grabbed me as if she was trying to stop that tear from falling. She gave me that big momma hug I needed, the hug I didn't even know I came for. She whispered in my ear that she trusted that I would make the right decision. "You a smart girl". The pressure.

The truth was, I didn't know If I would make the right decision. The decision was all the more harder because I simply, did not want to make one. I didn't want things to be this fucked up. It all happened so fast. How was I supposed to know that him, his family and his baby momma were all bat shit crazy? I didn't sign up for all this drama. I knew that I'd experienced more than most 20 year old's had, but I had never experienced this type of shit. Now I got beef that I did not even cause. Yet and still, he was trying so hard. He loved me so much, I was his reason to try, to care, to push. I knew leaving him would be one of the hardest things I had to do at this point. I was afraid. Hell, the last nigga I tried to leave threw me into a wall. See, they were two different types of crazy, but indeed crazy. I definitely didn't want to experience anything even close to that again. Teff had already shown me enough for me to know that simply telling him that I was leaving him was not an option. He had now made up in his mind that I was pregnant, even though all of the test he had stolen said negative. I knew I had to escape. I would have to figure out when he would be away and take all of my shit without getting caught. That task seemed impossible. Teff did not have a job, he always had my car and my phone. There was no sneaking with him. I could tell my daddy, but my daddy would just go straight to his ass. With the both of them being crazy, two different types of crazy, but indeed crazy, I didn't even want to image the confrontation between those two. I felt like my daddy would undoubtedly kill Teff if he knew all of the danger he had put me in. Also, I felt like Teff would try to kill my daddy from utter intimidation. I did not want to be the cause of any of that. Telling daddy was not an option.

Another major battle I was having was the fact that he really wasn't doing anything wrong at the moment, granted everything was already fucked up. What I meant by this was that he was really trying. He hadn't flipped out in a while and was so proud of it. He would even periodically say, "I'm doing good aren't I?" I would give him a big kiss and say, "Yes you are baby". As crazy as it may sound, I think he deserved credit for that. We had even gone down to the Social services department to get him Medicaid to purchase the meds he used to take before. I still loved him, but all of the craziness around us he had caused made me resent him. I felt like bad luck followed him and as long as I was around him, I would have it. I did not want him to think I did not love him or Miguel, I just wanted my life back. My simple, carefree, drama free, luck filled, Life! I was wrestling with this "Ride or Die" thing too. He told me I was his "Ride or Die". I took it as a major compliment. I knew that quitting was NOT the "Ride or Die" thing to do. I could hear him now;

"So, you just go quit on me huh? You never really loved me!"

I could see through his anger and feel his hurt. He needed someone not to leave him. His mom left him. I'm supposed to be the one that'll never do that to him. This boy loved my breath early in the morning, he did not even flinch when he picked up my snot tissue when I was sick, how could I just leave him? He is a man with unfortunate circumstances. I will never figure this out. Maybe I should pray....

Hey God,

Ok so you know, I still don't know how to pray like those ladies at church. Honestly, I don't want to. I don't think it matters anyway. Ok so you see all this crazy shit going on around me right? I need you to like, I don't know, do something to help me get out of it easy, like free and clear? Please. I need to leave him, things are bad, I know it's time to go. I'm a little scared though. I'm asking for you to protect me. I need you to make him do something to piss

*me off so I can be like "Ok, I'm leaving you because of this".
He not doing anything wrong right now, so I don't want to
be like I'm leaving for no reason, ya know? Can you give me
sign? Okay, so If something happens soon, I'll know it's time
to go. Okay cool! So, can you do that and make sure he don't
try to kill me or my people. Amen, I love you, thank you.....*

Meanwhile Teff needed a job. I thought that would solve a lot of our problems for a few reasons. I wouldn't be agitated from being broke all the time when I knew I didn't have to be. Reason two; I could have some fucking space damn! Alonzo made plans to come get Teff to take him job hunting. I was leaving out headed to the shop at the same time. I said, jokingly.

"Why don't yall take Blue Eyes and let me get the Lexus for the day". Alonzo threw me the keys too fast with no questions. The look on Teffs face told it all. I retracted that statement as fast as I could.

"I'm just kidding Alonzo".

He repeatedly asked me if I was sure. I was convinced Alonzo trying to get me killed!

A few days later I was at work when Alonzo called. I could tell he was shocked to hear my voice because Teff always had my phone. He asked where Teff was. I replied,

"Somewhere driving out my damn gas".

We both laughed. Then he goes on to say; stuttering a bit, may I add,

"Hey, I've been wanting to talk to you about something, but you know, ole boy always around."

I'm thinking "Here it goes, he's gonna hit on me in 5, 4,3, 2....

I replied a simple "Umm hum."

"Man, never mind, just tell Teff to hit me back"....Click.

Oh hell no. He ain't go leave me hanging like that. Redial.

"Alonzo! What the fuck?"

"Nah, everything all good, I shouldna even said shit, just tell Teff to ca…"

"Alonzo, if you hang up on me again Imma fuck you up!"

He let out a long sigh.

"Okay.................... all Imma say is.................. You a good girl, you don't deserve.....". Click.

Redial.

At this point I am pacing up and down the sidewalk from the salon to Mickies sucking down a Newport.

Screaming even louder than before,

"Alonzo! Don't you fucking hang up. What don't I deserve?"

"Look, I'll tell you when I see you, I don't wanna tell you over the phone".

"Aight, where you at?" He started to laugh.

"I'm serious, Imma meet you somewhere tonight".

"I'll be around, just hit me".

"Bet".

I needed to know this information asap. I was so anxious. All clues lead to him telling me about another bitch. I was a bit angry at the thought, and even the audacity, but not as angry as I would be if I had truly believed it. As many things as Teff was and was not, I was never concerned about him cheating. Teff worshipped the ground I walked on. He was way too far up my ass to be even the least bit concerned about another bitch. But what else could it be? Hell, I knew everything else. I was so nervous and running low on time. Teff would be on the way to the shop at any second. I had better make my plans before he came. I called Chi Chi. I explained to her what happened and that I planned to lie on her to get away, so, stick to the script. Of course, she agreed. She was excellent about stuff like this. I erased all of their phone calls out of my call log as well. Yes, Teff was on my ass like that. I knew the fool I was dealing with. Getting caught in a lie with Teff was not what I was prepared to deal with. I had all of my lies in order, and it was settled.

I jumped in the car and kissed him like normal. We went to the house, and I got ready for bed as usual. Chi Chi was set to call me around 8. The phone rang at 8:03 p.m. He answered of course and apparently, she used her good acting skills because when Teff handed me the phone, he whispered that she sounded like she was crying.

He was always ear hustling so I could only pray that she stuck to the script as directed.

"What's wrong Chi? Who Trey? Calm down. Stop crying, I can barely understand you. Please don't do that. I'm coming right now!"

Teff was all ears.

"Chi Chi aight?"

I quickly jumped up, ran to the back room and slipped on some jeans. I yelled from the back room,

"No, this nigga got her talking bout she about to take a bunch of pills".

I threw on a sweatshirt, but I stuffed a cute shirt in my purse. The perks of being a size 3.

"You about to go over there?"

"Hell yeah, she needs me, you stay here with the baby, I'll be back".

I got the fuck out of there before this nigga had a chance to think any harder and stop me, or even worse, try to come.

I was out. Whew. I immediately called Alonzo.

"I'm in route, where you at?"

He laughed hysterically.

"You wasn't playing was you?"

"Hell no, I gots to know what the fuck is going on".

He told me to meet him at the crib and we'd go from there. So that's what I did. I called Chi Chi to confirm that the plan had worked and my whereabouts. I quickly fell back into the place I had been that day I drove Alonzo's car to Mcdonalds. I enjoyed my weird combination of heat and cool wind as I blasted the tweet cd Teff had stolen for me. I felt like a rebel sneaking off as I drove with my knee,

I took off my sweatshirt, while my blunt blew out in the ash tray. I thought about how things would be if I left him. This thought gave me an extremely free feeling followed by an extreme fear. Would I really be free even if I left? I just could not wrap my mind around him being ok with my leaving. I really could not be sure if he would simply be pitiful or try to kill me. On that note I popped another cigarette in my mouth and called Alonzo as I pulled in his driveway. He walked out, opened his passenger door and gestured for me to get in.

I didn't know where we were going, and I didn't ask. I didn't care. I needed to hear this information, this secret that caused me to just about risk my life to hear. If Teff found out, he'd kill me. It was worth it. We pulled up to an empty lot, which seemed to me like it was the middle of nowhere. I stared at Alonzo, and he stared straight out the window. He seemed so nervous; he was usually so smooth. He would not even look at me until he offered me a drink. After a about another minute of complete silence other than the sound of a very close plane , I screamed,

"Alonzo!!!"

"Huh?"

"Tell me!!!"

We both lit our cigarettes.

"I am, I'm sorry, I'm just a little nervous".

"Nervous for what Alonzooooo?" I dragged his name out to express my frustration.

"I just didn't think you would really come."

"Well, you wouldn't tell me on the phone, what the fuck was I supposed to do? So come on wit it".

I appeared completely unbothered, but I was trembling inside. Yes, Teff was this and Teff was that, but I loved that boy. I was almost sure that what he was about to say was going to break my heart, I mean, what else could it be? He was either on drugs, had a disease or he was cheating. I pulled my cigarette extra hard and squinted my eyes as if it would protect me from a hard hit as I listened to him fumble around with his words.

"So, you remember that day I came to take Teff job hunting?"

"Yeah."

"Well, you know, I had no idea, where he wanted to go or whatever............" He paused and continued to sip and smoke his cigarette.

I wanted to kill him. He was talking super slow and saying a lot of nothing.

"Well, he had other plans............I kept saying, "Man, ain't you supposed to be looking for a job?" But you know, It wasn't go seem right for me to tell him not to or tell him straight up no, cause then he was go be looking at me funny............I tried to stall as long as I could but............"

"So, he cheating on me? What's huh name?"

"See that's the crazy part, he had it all lined up. It was more than one. He had the numbers and the addresses ready. I was like damn dude, why are you doing this? You got this beautiful girl at home........"

"I don't wanna hear no more".

I felt like I was going to cry for maybe one whole minute, then that all turned into rage!

"So, you mean to tell me, I been in out of court to help this nigga take his baby, this bitch done keyed my car, she be sitting outside my fucking house when I get home, his momma crazy, he crazy!! I been spending all my money cause this nigga don't have no muthafucking job and you cheating? You cheating? Fuck that shit!" I yelled at him like he did it. I was shooting the messenger and had no apologies.

"You need some money?"

"You got these bitches numbers?"

He handed me his phone.

I attempted to call two of the numbers which resulted in two voicemails. I was livid. I lit another cigarette and reached for the bottle of Grey Goose that sat between his legs, searching on what to do with my feelings, when it hit me.

"That's it!" I said as I grabbed my phone.

"Huh, whats it?"

"This is it". I looked him in his eyes as I shook my head yes smiling like I'd just found the answer key to my test.

I Instantly I felt a sense of.....This is on purpose. I knew that this was the answer to what I had prayed about. Although I didn't expect it to happen this way, I really didn't know what I expected, but I had that feeling. A feeling that assured me that this was all wrong, but it was still all RIGHT! I called my daddy.

I had to convince my daddy to let me use his truck without him actually knowing what I was using it for. Good luck with that. My daddy asked a million question. You could not hide shit from him. Even when I lied, he always knew. This man just did an eight-year bid, couldn't too much get past him. But I tried anyway.

"Daddy....hey daddy."

"Hey baby".

What you doing tomorrow?"

"I gotta work, why, what's up?"

"What time you work?"

"Nah, what's up?"

I took a deep breath.

"Can I drive your truck tomorrow?"

"Use my truck, for what?"

"I just need to move some stuff".

He paused for a while. I knew he was figuring me out. Just say yes daddy please, I thought. I held my breath.

"It's a stick, remember, can you drive a stick?"

"Damn, no, damn I forgot." I looked at Alonzo and whispered, "Can you drive a stick?"

He shook his head no.

"Ok daddy, don't worry about it then".

"Nah, what the hell going on. Where you at? Who you talking to?"

"I'm with my friend, I'm not home".

"Where Teff?"

I raised my voice a little.

"He at home, daddy Imma call you back."

".............. Aight".

Ugh, that was so stressful, I regretted calling him, now he was on radar. I didn't have many options. I had an ass load of shit to get outta this house in a small period of time. Teff had to go see his probation officer at 1 p.m. the next day. I knew he would try to make me stay but I would give him a good excuse to leave. Then I would have to clear the house out as much as I could while he thought I was coming back to get him. I did not expect Alonzo to help. No one else really knew the situation enough to help other than my crazy ass brothers. I did not want to involve them. Plus, I would have to get them which would take up space in my litte car that I needed. My oneand only ally was Chi Chi. I knew that Chi Chi would lie and say she's coming and not show up for something that she really did not want to do but with this situation, she'd come. I did not have to question that much, but I needed to threaten her to assure my request.

I called Chi Chi and quickly gave her the rundown of what I'd just found out from Alonzo, then the game plan for the following day. Chi Chi had the tendency to be late so even though Teff had to be dropped off at 1 p.m., I told her to meet me at 1 p.m. as well. Then I sealed the conversation with this.

"Chi Chi, I need you to meet me at one o'clock".

"Okay, Nika, I'll be there".

"If you don't meet me at one, I'm never talking to you again".

I think she understood how serious I was. Hell, she had just threatened me about leaving. Why wouldn't she help me?

I had run into my homeboy Moe at the store when I stopped for cigarettes on the way to Alonzo's. I used to braid his hair at my crib before I began working at the shop. He said he had lost my number. When he asked me how I was doing, I noticed he had a rather large car. A caprice classic to be exact. I briefly told him that I was in a fucked-up situation and that I may need his assistance. He seemed concerned and willing to help. He even mentioned that he had a trailer that he used for to pull his bike. Perfect. I called him and explained that I needed him to show up with the trailer at 1pm the next day. He said, "No doubt".

It was set. I could feel my freedom coming. It felt great. However, I was unsure of what to do for that night. Although I had a poker face for the most part. In this situation, I would blow it. I knew that I could not go back to the crib, get in the bed, and pretend one that I didn't know that he was doing me so dirty and two, that I had these brilliant plans to come forth the next day without blowing my cover. I was afraid to fall out with him because now he had begun this "Give me my key back" thing when he'd get mad. It would piss me off so bad because, nigga, you need me. Everything in that house was mine except his raggedy ass pull out couch he'd found that we slept on. This further showed me just how crazy he was because most niggas would have some act right just because they knew they didn't have shit. Not this nigga. I could not go back tonight. I would just tell him It got late so I feel asleep at Chi Chi's. Hell, I couldn't call him. He didn't have a phone or car and he had the baby. Even if he did come looking for me, he didn't know where Chi Chi lived anyway. I would simply hide my car and go home. I knew my daddy was out hoeing so my apartment was empty.

Alonzo did not say a word the entire time I set up my plan.

"So, you leaving?' I didn't know you was having all them other issues with him, I just thought the nigga didn't have no bread".

"It's so much. I'm done. And we go celebrate. Tomorrow night, me you and Chi Chi."

"Okay, we can do dat, what you wanna do now?"

"Take me back to my car, I'm going to my house tonight."

"So, you got your own crib?"

"Yep, I stayed with Teff because I wanted to be with him. I let my dad stay there but it's still my shit. He be at my momma house all the time anyway."

"You go be good by yourself?"

"Yeah, I'll be fine, I can't go lay in the bed with that nigga tonight, I ain't go act right."

Alonzo drove me back to his house. He asked me for a hug. His hug was inappropriate, for a friend. He asked if I needed him to follow me. I told him that it was up to him but assured him I was good either way. He followed me of course. We hid our cars in the parking lot of the building beside mine. He walked me inside. It was awkward. My emotions were very much disturbed, and I was quite tipsy. He came in and we finished the bottle of grey goose. I showed him around my two-bedroom apartment as if it was a mansion to take the edge off of us sitting there looking at each other. Now we are in my room. I showed him my shelf. I had a sacred shelf of memories which consisted of everything that meant something to me. Letters, stuffed animals from my daddy and obituaries of everyone whom I've loved whomed passed away. I used entertaining to relax me because I was nervous as fuck. I had not been in my own apartment alone in so long made me nervous. I had been M.I.A. for months. My neighbor's, my boys did not even know what I had going on enough to even look out. I was not exactly sure why Alonzo was lingering, but I could guess.

"I just want you to be okay ".

"What you mean? I'm okay" I replied defensively.

Next thing you know he was kissing me. It was a good kiss. I found myself kissing him back as he attempted to lay me on my bed.

"Alonzo, what you doing?"

He didn't say a word as he pulled my pants down, followed by my panties. I felt the wetness of his tongue as he took a mouthful of my pussy. I let out a loud moan. I wanted to enjoy it; it was something to enjoy. However, the better it felt, the more nervous I became. I simply could not relax. I wrestled with how good his tongue felt and how if Teff showed up, how dead we'd both be. I wanted to take off running. I eventually pushed his head away from in between my legs.

"Alonzo, I'm scared".

"I ain't go let nothing happen to you."

He pulled his gun from his hip and laid it on the bed beside us. Then he put on a condom and proceeded to push himself inside me. It felt so good. I thought to myself "You deserve this, he deserved this." After I struggled to enjoy a few more strokes, I pushed him all the way out and off of me.

"I can't do this."

"Please Baby, damn, it's so good."

Then he looked at me and noticed my physical state.

"Yo, are you shaking?"

I just stared at him, shaking reaching for a cigarette.

"You scared for real?"

"I want you to leave, he might come over here."

He had this shocked and disgusted look on his face.

"Damn, what that nigga do to you?"

I didn't say a word. He slowly but surely got dressed and I walked him to the door. He gave me a hug, stood back and shook his head.

"I'll be over tomorrow if you still want me to come. Maybe then you'll wanna fuck wit a real nigga."

I didn't say a word. I closed the door and walked my embarrassed ass to my bed. I had a long day ahead of me.

CHAPTER 11

DON'T LOOK BACK.
October 3rd, 2002

I slept like a baby surprisingly. It was morning and I was nervous as shit. I knew Teff was going to be pissed. I headed that way to pick up Miguel for daycare. I did not shower, and I wore the same clothes I left in so that he did not think I had been home. I had one client that morning and I had a break which was when I planned to take him to see his probation officer. He had a bad attitude and of course he questioned my whereabouts. I explained that I would drop Miguel off on my way to the shop. He assumed that I forgot about his appointment. Definitely not. I told him I'd be right back after my client. He did not like that either. He followed me around the house and watched me like hawk. He mentioned that he had talked to A.B. and that they were cool. Cool? I did not have time to investigate anymore of Teffs Drama. I really didn't give a fuck. I could smell my freedom and I refused to get distracted. I moved around really fast to get him away from me. As I got dressed, I scanned the house for all of my belongings. I secretly divided the dirty clothes pile, pretending to get them ready to wash. I gathered all of my scattered items as if I were cleaning up. I needed to be able to grab my things quickly and go. I desperately wanted to take all of my things, but I was willing to settle for what was important, so that is what I focused on.

I tried really hard not to be suspicious, but everything was suspicious to Teff. Just before I walked out the door, he stepped in front of the door and looked me up and down.

"What?"

"You up to something".

"Teff, what are you talking about?"

"I know you like the back of my hand".

He had this crazy grin on his face as if he caught me in a lie. I pretended to be totally confused.

"Teff, what are you talking about?"

"Give me my key" and snatched them out of my hand.

My worst nightmare had been realized. Out of all days, why today? I could not blow this. I was not giving up those keys today. Not without my shit. This had to end today. I was determined. This was my only chance. There were so many things that had to go right today, and it was already unraveling in the beginning. My heart sank down to my stomach. Think fast Nika. Get out of this. It was time to pull out the big guns. I began to cry. I shocked myself because I didn't even believe I could do it or make it seem real, but desperate times caused for desperate measures.

"Why do you always do this Teff? How would you feel if you lived with me and every time I got mad at you I made you give me your keys? How would you fee....." I began to cry even harder than before.

His reaction was hard to read. I could tell that half of him wanted to have some remorse, but the other half of him was crazy. I guess he wasn't that crazy in this instance because I was indeed up to something, but there was no proof. I was innocent and I was sticking to my story. You will never guess what happened next. This nigga handed me my keys back, well, forced them back in my had rather rudely. That was fine with me. Look at God. I fought back the grin that warmed up inside. I gave him a kiss goodbye and I was out of there. Whew, that was close.

Part one of my plan was completed, which was to come home after that all-nighter and face him. Now I just had a few more steps;

Make some money

Drop his ass off

Get my shit

Get Symone

And celebrate.

I was almost there.

The ride to the probation officer building was uncomfortably quiet. As we pulled up, he asked me was I going to come in with him. I explained that I needed to go around the corner and pay my light bill for my dad and that it didn't make any sense for me to come in there and sit there when I could be standing in line at the Duke Power place. Of course, he had a major problem with that idea. He hopped out of the car and slammed the door as hard as he could. I was sure that he had broken my window, I even flinched.

"You fucking lying. You a lying bitch".

I just pulled off.

It was 12:57. I jumped on the highway and drove as fast as my car would go. I was shaking, and so was my car. But I didn't look back. I was on a mission that seemed impossible. I just knew that this was my only chance. I couldn't image things getting any worse, but I knew that it would if I stayed. I had no other choice, and I was not sorry. *Something had told me, if I didn't take this chance, there would be no more.* I swing Blue Eyes into a parking space like a bat out of hell. I damn near pulled the keys out the car before I had it all the way in park. It was 1:06. Where the hell was Chi Chi? I lit my piece of blunt and hit it as I climbed the stairs. It seemed as if they had doubled.

My legs felt as if they would collapse from under my body, I was trembling. Then the phone rang. It read A.B.. I started not to answer, but then I thought, let me see who this is. I tried to calm the shakiness in my voice as I said hello...I was almost completely out of breath.

"Where you at"? It was Teff!

"At the Duke Power place like I replied."

"Well come back and get me, my probation officer ain't here".

"Ok I'm coming, I'm in line".

He paused, then he hung up, which scared the complete shit out of me because it was clear that he was pissed, and he knew I was lying, which meant he was coming, and I was alone. My mind was racing. Was he coming? Why the hell did he have A.B.'s phone? He hated him.

I walked in the house and took a deep breath looking around at the work I had ahead of me and the small amount of time I had. First agenda was to find his gun. He couldn't have taken it with him to the probation officers, or could he? I planned to take it with me. I wasn't going to piss this nigga off and leave him with a gun. He wasn't going to use it on me, I was going to use it on him if anyone was going to use it.. I'd never shot a gun, but I'd learn. I looked in every spot he had ever hidden it and some others. Nothing. Time was ticking, I could not waste any more time. I began dragging baskets and trash bags full of clothes to the front door and kicked them down the stairs. Then I ran down the stairs jumped over the pile and packed my car from top to bottom. Next thing you know, my car was full to the point I could barely get in to drive. I was sweaty, out of breath and my heart was beating so fast I felt that I just may have a heart attack.

Chi Chi wasn't there or answering the phone. I lit a cigarette and paced the sidewalk as I called Moe with the caprice. I thought damn, "Where the hell is Chi Chi?." Before the thought completely went through, I saw that black Honda turn the corner like another bat out of hell. I had never been so happy to see her as I was at that moment. "Come on bitch"! We ran up the stairs and I showed her what to get. Dishes, vacuum cleaner, microwave, toys, all kinds of stuff. Just as we had filled her car to its complete compacity, Teff began to call my phone back-to-back. *Something told me to forget the rest and leave.* Besides, there was no way I could get a crib, daybed, 32' T.V., bike or my daughter's kitchen set in the car anyway and it was clear that Moe wasn't going to show up. We hauled ass to the highway straight to the eastside, where I belonged.

1:32 p.m.

As soon as my wheels touched the highway, Teff called again. This time he left a message.

'Whyyyyy. Why boo? You took....you took everything! What I do to deserve this?"

I immediately called Chi Chi laughing.

"Bitch, why this nigga just called me crying talking about "What I do to deserve this?" Mutherfucker please, you dragging me through hell, and you think you go cheat? Fuck that nigga!"

"Damn right fuck him, you about to get back to your life".

"Hell yeah."

My daddy did not completely live at my place. He basically used it as his storage and a place to go when he did not want to be with one of his hoes now that he was done with my mom. I decided to give him a call just before we pulled up. You know, just in case he was in the middle of some shit I should not see.

He walked outside just as Chi Chi and I pulled up. He had on no shirt, some pajama pants, and a house coat walking on the back of bedroom shoes. I loved him. I gave him the biggest grin as I hoped out of the car and hugged him.

"I'm hoooome!"

He stared at the overflow of crap in our cars.

"What the hell going on? He said ginning, he was always grinning.

"Nothing, I'm home daddy, I'm back".

"Ah hell nah, something happened?".

"I'm leaving that mutherfucka".

He laughed with us then proceeded to ask,

"He didn't put his hands on you or no shit like that did he?"

"Nope".

"Aight , cool".

Then he began to help us unload our cars. As soon as we got settled, we proceeded to get high.

I explained to my dad about how I was just tired of his shit, but not trying to tell him too much. Teff called repeatedly and left messages almost each time.

The first message said;

"You better get over here and get all this shit right now. If you don't be over here by......Three o'clock Imma throw all this shit out the fucking window. This T.V., this bike, this kitchen set, all this shit!"

"Daddy, said he go throw my T.V. out the window!"

"I'll buy you another one".

Each message was as different as night and day.

The next one said;

"Boo, I love you, I'm not go throw your shit out the window, just come over here and talk to me, please.

Then the next;

"Fuck you bitch, you ain't shit, yo pussy wasn't right last time I fucked you. I know you been fucking somebody else. Hoe!"

Then another;

"And you better not send yo peoples over here cause can't none of them muthafuckas hold me. I got something for all of em. Ya daddy, ya brothers. All of em can get it. Fuck all of em!'

"Daaaadddy! He said he go fuck yall up".

"As long as he didn't put his hands on you, I'm good. He just mad right now I'm not in it. I gotta learn to stay out of your shit. You a grown-ass woman.

"Daddy, he talking shit though!"

I so wanted my daddy to beat his ass. What the fuck? So now he decides to be a normal daddy? Then he made it even worse saying; "I kinda like that boy".

Meanwhile Teff continued with leaving messages. The next one said;

"I don't want no beef whicho peoples. I ain't go do nothing to your stuff. Just....just, call me back boo".

3:02 p.m.

Fuck that nigga. He was clearly crazy, and I was gone. I had things to do, not to mention a celebration that night. Chi Chi and I had food and drinks at Applebees, then went our separate ways. I picked up Symone and took her to her WIC appointment. Just before I headed home, Shelia called me and said Teff told her one, I had left him and two; that I had taken some of his things with me. I had accidently taken a bag of his clothes during my rush. I agreed to meet her at the salon to return his items. She gave me the biggest hug.

"What happened Nika?"

I paused for a while. I wanted to choose my words correctly for three reasons, the first being that I knew nobody would be ok with you telling them that their child was simply batshit crazy. The second reason was that no one wants to hear that they are indeed the reason why their child was batshit crazy. Reason three was she would go and tell him everything I said and then he would get roweled up again and at the moment, he seemed to be calm.

"Shelia, I am not happy".

She paused for a while. I could tell she could not find a rebuttal to that statement.

"Well, I wouldn't ask you to be unhappy for my son. I just need to make sure you're serious, because if you're not serious.......He can't deal with this, don't do this if you're not serious".

"I'm serious Shelia".

She looked so disappointed.

"Ok, well, you still my daughter so you better still call me".

She grabbed me for another hug.

"Okay, I will", I assured her smiling.

"And you still go do my hair".

She began to laugh and she added;

"Teff said he don't know how the hell them two little girls got all the shit out the house that fast".

We both laughed as I reached into the car and handed her the bag full of his clothes. I realized she had picked Miguel up from daycare to take him home. I opened to door and kissed Miguel.

"Damn, Imma miss you".

6:45 p.m.

I happily headed home. It had been a long day. I wanted to chill for a bit before Alonzo and Chi Chi came over. I slipped into comfortable clothes and tended to Symone. I tried to watch some T.V., but my phone would not let me great. The phone was across the room by the patio because of the bad reception so every time it rang, I had to get up to look. Teff continued to call repeatedly. Then Shelia.

"Hey ma".

"This muthafucka talking about he gave Miguel back to Saleena".

"Huh? He hates her".

"That's what I thought too. I told him don't ever call me again. After all we done been through to take Miguel from that bitch, he just go give him back just like that!"

She was screaming and I was quiet with confusion. Until I remembered something he had said during one of his rants.

"He told me that if I ever left him, he was gonna give the baby back to Saleena and move back to Boston."

"He a goddamn lie, he not allowed to go back to Boston, he banned from Boston! That's why he here now. They made him move to Charlotte with me, that's part of his probation!"

Well damn. Banned from Boston? Well, he did beat up a cop and take his gun. That's a good reason to be banned from a place. So, if what he said could not be true, why did he give the baby back? I knew for a fact he hated Saleena. He would do anything to keep Miguel from her. He must really be losing it.

As I sat and tried to rationalize Shelia's and my conversation, Chi Chi called.

"I need you to please answer the phone for this mutherfucka cause now he calling my damn phone!"

"Huh?"

"I'm on a fucking date and he calling my phone back-to-back, and he leaving messages".

"Wow".

"Imma give you my voicemail code, he sound real crazy. You need to hear one of these messages he left cause it ain't right Niq."

As I tried to dial Chi Chi's number to listen to her voicemail my daddy called.

"Yo, so what you got going on with this nigga?

"What you mean?"

"I mean are you seriously done with him or you just mad?"

"I'm done daddy, why, he calling you too? He calling everybody. I don't even understand how he got everybody's number without my phone!".

"Yo, you think that nigga suicidal?"

"NOOO! He crazy, that's what he is. Why you say that?"

"Cause people call you confessing and apologizing for shit when they about to kill they damn self".

"Daddy he just want attention. He just doing this shit because he know you go call and tell me."

"Well go over there and holla at him, he say he just wanna talk to you and shit"

"No daddy".

"Why you just won't answer the phone so he can talk to you?'

I started yelling.

"You don't understand! It's a circle! Imma go over there, and he go sweet talk me then its go be the same shit again! I can't do it no more daddy! I'm not answering the phone and I'm not going over there. Its OVER!"

Aight, "he said rather calmly.

9ish

I got up to grab a cigarette. That "Aight" my daddy gave me wasn't the normal aight. It was that "You fucking up, aight". Why was he so emotional evolved when it came to this dude? He usually just wanted to threaten the shit out of any nigga I introduced him too. I couldn't believe that I just yelled at my daddy like that. He was my favorite person in the world, but I meant what I said. I was not talking to him. This shit was over, and no one could change my mind. No one truly knew what I was going through. Not even Chi Chi. I just wanted my life back and I was going to keep my foot down to get it! *Something inside of me would not let me fold even when my heart wanted to.* Nothing could make me answer or go over. Not even my daddy! I proceeded to call Chi Chi's voicemail again. One the first voice mail, he was just saying how my voicemail was full and he just wanted me to come over to talk to him tonight. Not! The next voicemail was different.

"I love you boo, just come to my funeral".

Here he goes with the crazy shit. Really Teff? You really go take it there? You fucked up and I am gone. Chill out. After all that shit you just talked, now you want me to come to your funeral? Nigga please.

Shortly after Sonya called. She said that Teff had called her too and that he asked could he come to the shop tomorrow and talk to me. She said that she told him yes as long as he behaved and wanted to make sure it was okay with me. I explained what all had happened during the course of that day. However, I told her that it was fine for him to come talk to me. I figured he couldn't do too much harm to me with her around. Chi Chi and Alonzo both called within minutes of each other to confirm they were on the way. I explained to Alonzo the events of the day as well. He asked if I still thought he should come. I told him hell yeah, this was my freedom celebration. He seemed unsure.

Shelia called again with worry in her voice.

"Have you talked to Teff?

"No, why?".

"I don't know what the fuck is going on with him, he just called wanting to talk to everyone in the house saying he love us and telling everyone bye, now he not answering the phone".

As soon as I began to get nervous, I was interrupted by him beeping in on the other line.

"Shelia, he fine, he calling me right now".

"Well, Imma send Chad and his uncle Miguel over there to check on him".

"Okay, Imma call Fred to go over there too".

Before I could call Fred, Chi Chi called again.

"Hey, Teff said could you erase some of your messages so he can leave something on your voice mail

"Aight".

"And unlock the door, I'm around the corner and Mariah sleep".

I unlocked the door, erased a message, then called Fred.

"Fred".

"Yoooo".

I gave him the rundown of the day and the phone call I just had with Shelia.

"Man, that nigga just need a blunt and a beer". He laughed.

"I don't know why yall doing this shit when you know yall go be right back together tomorrow. That nigga love you man and you love him. Cut this bullshit out".

"I'm for real Fred".

"Well, I hope you just mad, I like yall together. I'm around the corner, I'm about to go check on that nigga in a minute, I'm smoking a blunt wit yo pops".

Okay cool".

10:10p.m.

I watched as Teff called my phone again. I watched the phone ring. I watched it end and I watched the voicemail icon pop up. Shelia called again.

"Oh my God he shot his self in the head!"

Chi Chi walked in just as I dropped the phone. I had I blank stare on my face as I shook my head no.

"What's wrong Niq?", Chi Chi asked as she laid Mariah down on the couch.

"Shelia.....Shelia just said....Teff shot his self in the head".

"Hell no, give me the phone". I handed her the phone and walked to the kitchen to get a cigarette. I paced the floor back and forth with my eyes glued to Chi Chi.

"Call Fred, Fred was on the way over there, call Fred!"

She had the phone on speaker as is rang. I could not be still. My body trembled. I thought to myself, "I had to hear it wrong. She said leg, not head, he was fine", I told myself. He better be fine. I refused to let my mind go any further. I refused to accept anything less than that. I just need to confirm it so I could continue breathing.

"Hello!" Fred answered loudly.

"Fred, what the fuck going on? Shelia just called and said something crazy."

"I don't know, its ambulances, fire trucks and cops everywhere, hold on."

Hold on? Hold on? I couldn't hold on. I couldn't even breathe. I couldn't be still. I couldn't stop shaking, I definitely couldn't hold on! This was the longest hold in the world. We waited hearing all of the commotion in the background.

"Yo, they said the nigga dead, damn......he gone!"

Chi Chi turned toward me with the saddest look on her face.

"He gone NIq".

I hit the floor. I'm not sure what happened to my legs. They simply stopped working. I sat there on my floor in totally disbelief shaking my head back and forth, refusing to believe my ears. I could not make my mind nor heart except it. I smoked my cigarette down to the filter. Then the phone rang again.

It was Shelia.

"My son is dead". Click.

I just sat on the floor. Not because I didn't want to get up, but because my legs simply refused to operate. Chi Chi handed me the blunt. Before I could hit it a second time, she said with the most serious face I had ever seen her have,

"We gotta get the fuck outta here".

I continued to sit in the same spot on the floor with the same confused look on my face shaking my head from side to side telling myself that this is not happening. I continued to hit the blunt again and again until Chi Chi reappeared in front of me. Just realizing that she had even left my presence, I looked up at her from my gaze to hear her say,

"I'm about to put this stuff in the car, get up and get in the car and I got the babies."

"Why Chi Chi, where we going?"

"Nika, the way Shelia just called and said that shit, ain't no telling what she thinking or what she might do, she might be on her way over here now, she crazy let's go".

She had an arm full of clothes and other random items. I watched her disappear behind my front door as I tried to pull myself off the floor. I had finally stood up by the time she came back in to grab Mariah off the couch. I dragged my body to the car pausing to hit the blunt on the way. Before we could back the car up, my phone rang, and I went insane. I screamed,

"Turn it off! Turn that ringer off! I don't wanna ever hear that ringtone again!"

"Hey,......No she's right here beside me..... she's...... she's....okay.....okay, yeah I know, I got her, I'm taking her with me now. Oh wow....really?....Oh my God! Well, she will be with me, don't worry about that, okay hold on.

She turned and looked at me. I was already staring at her the entire time. I knew it was my daddy. He was always really loud like he was on speaker phone in his normal voice, but he was even louder this night. I heard every word. I wish I hadn't. He told Chi Chi about how crazy it was at the scene and about how he had burst through the crime scene tape to make sure I wasn't in there.

"It's your daddy". She tried to hand me the phone. I just looked at her and shook my head no.

"She don't wanna talk......yeah....right this shit is crazy". She turned to me and said, "He said he loves you".

I shook my head yes.

"She loves you too, ok, bye."

CHAPTER 12

IT WAS ALL A DREAM.
October 4th-9th 2002

Chi Chi took me to her aunt's house where she was staying until her apartment got ready. I went straight to bed and off to sleep. I slept like a baby. I was awakened by the bright light in the room the next morning. It was about noon. I told Chi Chi what I though was a dream, and she confirmed that it was not a dream. I threw the covers back over my head. It would be so much easier to sleep this way. Being awake required me to think and look what I had to think about. Upon Chi Chi's confirmation, I immediately started to feel the pain of my entire heart being ripped out of chest. The pain was so bad it had no words. I decided to hide under the covers while Chi Chi and I discussed the events of the night before. I cried like a baby. I did not want to talk about it, my answers were short. Not only did I not want to talk about it, but I also didn't want to move, eat, shower, get dressed, I did not want to exist. I just did not understand what the fuck I was to do with my life after THIS! So, I'm just supposed to bury my boyfriend and then go back to work and just drive around like I was doing before. No way. *There was no way my life could ever be the same or the least bit normal every again.* I cried even harder after that thought. I continued hide under the covers.

"So, what are you wearing tonight?"

I threw the covers from over my head all to give Chi Chi an are you crazy look.

"Tonight?"

"Yeah, Ducies birthday party".

"I ain't going to no fucking party!!!"

"Oh yes the fuck you are because I'm going and I'm not leaving you by yourself".

I continued to lay under the covers while Chi Chi showered. I heard Symone and Mariah playing in the next room. I knew I was in no position to deal with her. I called my grandma Anita and asked if Symone could stay with her a few days. She said yes of course. I managed to pull myself out of the bed and to the shower. We headed back to my apartment to pack up Symone and my things for the next few days. The next stop was Grandma Anita's house. I broke the news to my grandma. Although she had only met him once, she was very upset, and she assured me that Symone would be fine with her. Being that my grandma had no filter, I had to stress the point that Symone did not know what was going on and that I wanted to keep it that way. She agreed. I did not want to leave my baby. She was not hard for me to deal with at all. She was actually the sweetest kid I had ever encountered. However, I needed a minute to deal with this. I was in no position to mother. She did not deserve that. I knew she would get all she needed from my grandma and there my mom, dad and her Godmother had full access to her as well. I was not ready to deal with her questions. She loved Teff and I knew eventually she would ask where he was, and I would want to just die with him. He was a father to her. Plus, there was about to be a lot of smoking and drinking going on. I couldn't deal with any of that. I kissed my baby goodbye, then I cried in the car. The fact that I even had to do this was more weight on top of the reason why I was doing it. I did not even have an idea as to how long I needed, because I had never been through anything close to this before. I decided, I would take it a day at a time.

"I'll see you in a few days sugar".

Chi Chi and I sat in the car in my grandmas drive-way discussing how the blunt we were in the middle of smoking was the last one and we were both dead ass broke. We needed, weed, food and gas and of course Chi Chi had a plan. She told me that some guy and his friend wanted to take us to lunch. Perfect free food, however, there was one problem. My boyfriend just died, I didn't want to entertain, I didn't even want to talk. Chi Chi convinced me that it wouldn't be that bad and that she would make up a lie for us to leave quickly. I hadn't eaten anything since Applebee's the day before. Let me get this free meal. Hopefully, these guys weren't talkative.

First of all, the guys were ugly. I carried on with the best smile I could fake. I tried my best to stay engaged in what some would call a conversation with small talk. It may not have been as bad as I felt it was. At this point he could have been the man of my dreams and I would not be able to see it. I did not want any part of this but the food and only enough to stop the hunger, because fuck food. My life was over, my baby was dead, it was my fault, and I just gave my daughter to my 77-year-old grandma, I just wanted to go home, but then again, not so much. Home was scary as well. I wanted to be left alone, but not completely alone. I was not exactly sure of what I wanted but I knew I did not want to be at Outback with these niggas. Just when I thought things could not get any worse, they did. The waiter asked how with the check would be divided. These motherfuckers asked for 4 separate checks. I fought hard not to show any expression of my face. How the fuck are you going to invite us to dinner, and not pay for it? Before I had a chance to overthink it Chi Chi fixed it all by saying one sentence.

"Nika let me out, I need to go to the bathroom". I smiled inside as I added. "I need to go too".

We began talking shit as soon as the bathroom door closed.

"We walking the fuck outta here", Chi Chi insisted.

"I'm wit it".

We were off. We didn't even walk too fast. We were blocks away before their stupid ass even realized we were gone.

We weren't hungry but still, very broke. Chi Chi ALWAYS had a solution, that's why I fucked with her the long way. Now, although radical, it was still indeed, a solution.

"I have a way for us to get $300 but I'm a little nervous about it, that's why I ain't said nothing about it".

I just looked at her.

"We can do a house call".

"What the fuck is a house call Chi Chi?"

"So, I talked to this old ass white guy earlier, I told him everything, he picked out a girl, he knows its $300, but..."

"Whhhaaat! But What?

"We gotta go to his house!"

"Oh my God, that don't sound right, where he stay?"

"See that's the thing, we gotta find it, I have an idea, I have the address".

"Fuck it".

"Oh yeeeaaaah!!!"

We sought off into the darkness with an address, a lot of hope and little fear. We were low on gas, and we were out in west bubble fuck. The neighborhood was full of beautiful houses, well as much as we could see of them because there were no streetlights. We looked suspicious as hell, creeping around because he had absolutely idea where this house was, but we were smart. We followed the directions we were given. We could not call him because there was no longer any signal on our cricket phones. We finally reached the correct street and stopped at each house on it looking for the address. There it was.

My heart began to pound, and bad thoughts flew through my head.

"Chi Chi, you got a knife?"

"No".

"Bitch you got a fork? Something?"

She laughed hysterically.

"What you scared he go do something to me?"

"Yeah bitch, our phones don't even work, how you go get the money from him?!"

"Imma go up to the door and he go put it in my hand", she said calmly with a smirk on her face which turned into more laughter.

I just looked at her as she laughed at me.

"What if he grab you, what the fuck I'm supposed to do without a fork?'

"He not go grab me, you just stay in the car and keep your head turned because he asked for a blonde".

I just shook my head as she pulled to the bottom end of his circular driveway. The house was beautiful.

"Keep your head turned forward, and chill out".

She hoped out of the car with no fear. I stared at her though the rearview mirror as I felt around in her arm rest and glove compartment looking for something sharp, like a fork. She rang the doorbell, quickly an old white guy appeared. I studied their body language. Everything seemed all good. Next thing you know, the man disappeared, and I see Chi Chi running like hell toward the car. I reached over to crank up the car and swung open the door. She jumped in and pulled off like a bat out hell laughing hysterically. I just looked at her like "If you don't start talking bitch".

"This stupid motherfucker handed me his I.D. and the money and said "Ooo, let me show you the cool new condoms I bought", I burned out".

We both laughed agreeing that this was too easy. We got gas, got dressed and headed to Kings and Queens for Ducie's party. I wore all black, because I was a widow.

Ducie and his friends greeted us in the front. Ducie quickly noticed that I was in a rather dark mood. He asked Chi Chi what was wrong, and she gave a brief synopsis of my dilemmas. I watched his face become filled with sympathy.

"Nika baby what you drinking?".

I shrugged my shoulders.

"Grey goose? Let me get a bottle of grey goose", he said to the lady at the bar, then told us to follow him. He had a rather smoky section in the back. As soon as I sat down someone handed be a blunt. I had a bottle of grey goose in front of me and a gang of niggas staring at me. I drank, I smoked. This guy asked me why I looked so sad, so I told him, "My boyfriend shot his self in the head last night", which prompted him to hand me another blunt and pour me another drink. And this continued for a few hours until I found myself trying to get up off the floor in the bathroom, but I was still laughing. Despite it all, I ended up actually having a good time. Now it was time to get home. Chi Chi and I held each other up as we stumbled to the car.

"Girl you go have to drive, I'm too fucked up."

Chi Chi screamed "I can't drive!"

We reached our arms across the top of her black Honda civic and prayed".

When I woke up, we were parked sideways in front of my apartment. Chi Chi was out cold. Chi Chi woke up when I began to search for my phone and my keys. I found my keys, not my phone. "Fuck that phone". I needed to get in the house. Chi Chi climbed in my bed as I dry-heaved on the floor beside her. It happened. I spilled my guts on the floor and it felt great. Now I was halfway sure that I wasn't going to die. Chi Chi just laid there looking at me in pity.

"I want to help you, but I'm scared to move".

I managed to stubble to the bathroom to clean up and back to the bed where we both slept well into the next day.

Saturday October 5th

I woke up looking for my phone which I found in Chi Chi's car in the back seat. How? I had a million missed calls. Most of them from Shelia. I was afraid to speak to her. What would I say? I knew she hated me now, but I still wanted her to love me. Was this even possible? I made her son kill his self; I do not think I would love me anymore either. I was sorry. I felt too bad about it myself, I do not think it is possible for it to get any worse. But see, this is Shelia we're dealing with right now. Ain't no telling what this bitch might say to me, she was the craziest woman I'd meet. I was more afraid to call her back than anything I'd ever been afraid of. I consulted withChi Chi. She gave me the okay. This bitch didn't even say hello.

"I don't know which one of yall muthafuckas triggered him off, you, Saleena or your daddy, but the police are investigating!

"Wait a min, so he didn't kill his self?"

 Chi Chi was all ears.

"My son did not kill his self!!".

"Oh my god, well can you tell me about the investigation, because if someone killed him, I need to know".

"Nika, your daddy probably did it."

"No, he didn't, why are you saying that?"

"Because he was afraid of your daddy".

"That don't mean he killed him!"

"Saleena hated him too, hell, I don't know, but son did not kill his self."

"Okay". Click.

"Shes crazy".

She was only blaming my dad because things apparently didn't go the way she wanted with him. I knew their hooking up would cause problems. She was taking things too far. All signs pointed to suicide. Was she serious about this so-called investigation or was this just more drama, because I definitely didn't need anymore.

I looked a Chi Chi and shook my head.

""Ain't nobody kill Teff. She tripping. Hell, you have a million messages".

"He left another one." I added quickly.

"Huh?"

He left the last one and I never listened to it, I'm scared."

"You want me to listen to it with you?"

I shook my head yes as I called my voicemail. We had to listen to all of them because I never erased the other ones. it was the eeriest feeling hearing his voice and it was awful listening to him talk shit to me the way he did. I don't think a word exist to describe the way I felt listening to those messages. It was some odd combination of, love, fear, pain, guilt, disbelief.... I could go on and on.

The Message

Nika, I love you. I'm sorry I couldn't be the man you needed me to be. Tell my momma I love her and I'm sorry I couldn't be the son she needed me to be. Tell Symone, I love her. Whatever you do, just don't blame yourself, this is not your fault. Don't blame yourself. Just pay your respects when the time come and please please, please, don't kill my baby.

Now, I was back in my funk. Stuck in my thoughts, overwhelmed with hurt, no longer distracted by Grey Goose and weed. I was sober. It felt like I had been ran over by a tractor trailer and the hospital meds had worn off.

I decided to call Sonya. I had not talked to her since the *October 3rd.*

"Hey Nika, I was just thinking about you. How you doing?"

"Teff died Sonya."

"What!!?? No way Niq I just talked to him! When Nika?"

"The other night after you talked to him."

"But Nika, He was fine, he sounded fine, I told him he could come to the shop and everything."

"Sonya, he gone."

"Oh my God Nika, that coulda been you".

It could have been me? What did she mean? Could Teff have killed me? Would he? He loved me, right? Tears flowed rapidly as the reality set in. He literally called everyone to get me to come over. What if I would have gone? What if I would have listened to everyone and simply, gone over. One of three things would have happened;

I would have arrived at the apartment, with Symone, and found him, dead.

I would have arrived at the apartment, with Symone, and he would have killed himself in front of me.

Or

I would have arrived at the apartment, with Symone, and he would have killed me in front of Symone or killed us both and then killed himself or not.

He always told me if he, could not have me, no one would.

The bottom line is, it would have been even more horrible than it already was.

Just when I didn't think I could have a crazier thought.

It was Saturday and Chi Chi had to move. I was in no shape, and I did not have to tell her. You could look at me and tell. I sat on the floor against the wall in the corner in her new empty apartment like a little crazy person smoking blunt after blunt. I watched Chi Chi's things being bought in by people I think I knew but could not be sure because I was indeed, fucked up. I did not cry a lot or even hard because I was so high, I was almost numb. If my high came down too much, tears would roll down my face, then Chi Chi would roll another. I am not sure where all this weed was coming from because I did not have anything but myself.

I was like a zombie. I had no desire to eat, chew or anything of that nature. I had to push myself to get up and go to the bathroom and that was when I was about to pee on myself because I had waited until the very last minute. I had nothing to say. Chi Chi would periodically turn the shower on and tell me to get in, I would. She would buy me food and say "Eat Nika." Sometimes I would eat one or two. Chi Chi would invite various friends over (whom always had weed) and they would try having small talk with me, but I would just stare at them until they were creeped out. Chi Chi would then have to tell them,

"She's, she's not in the best mood right now", not sure of exactly what to say.

Poor Chi Chi, she was afraid to bring it up, she didn't know what to say to me. So, she didn't. She just let me be, and that's what I needed. I didn't want anybody asking me if I was ok every five minutes. I was not okay and that was a fact. I had no desire to do much of anything but stare at the wall and smoke, and that's all I did, oh and I would reach for the blunt and nod yes or no sometimes. I hated music. Every song reminded me of him, and I would lose it, so we would ride in silence. I stayed with Chi Chi in her new apartment. Staying at my apartment was not even an option and no discussion was required. Chi Chi handled my phone and my calls. The ringer was off, the ringtone made me want to die. As people found out ,my phone buzzed constantly. I had no capacity to deal with any of it. I finally decided to grab it to see Shelia calling. I answered.

"My son did not kill his self BITCH! One of yall muthafuckas did it and the police are investigating! Its either you and ya daddy or Saleena. One of yall killed my son and your gonna pay!"

I just cried silently. The few words I wanted to say couldn't get pass my cry to be heard. I was so heart broken. I loved Shelia. I called her mom. How could she be this mean to me? I didn't kill Teff. I wish this was all a long nightmare. Everyone hated me because this was all my fault. I may as well die too. I looked up to Chi Chi walk toward me quite aggressively with her hand reaching out toward the phone.

"Who you on the phone with?"

Before I could answer, she snatched the phone from my ear.

"Listen bitch, you go stop calling my friend with this bullshit cause I'll come over there and whoop yo ass bitch!" She got quite for a min, the continued with "Yeah whatever, we know he killed his self because of the message he left!"

Next thing you know she whispered to me "Can I please give them your voicemail code so they can hear these messages?" I shook my head yes.

Chi Chi talked shit the entire 5 mins it took for them to listen to the messages and continued as Shelia was calling back!

" I bet she feel stupid, calling over here with that bullshit!"

"Hey Shanika, ummm, I listened to all of the messages and, my son died at 10:10. He left the last message at 10:09, you were the last one he called, he really loved you. I let the whole family listen to it.".

I just listened.

"We're trying to figure out how we're going to bury him because the life insurance I had on him doesn't cover suicide. I'm having a hard time contacting his father's side of the family in Boston. We may have to cremate him.

"He said, come to my funeral".

"I know but we gotta come up with $500 just to cremate him and we don't even have that yet.

I began to cry. He wanted a funeral, he said it and there was nothing I could do to fix it for him. I had nothing. I continued to listen, unable to speak.

"We'll we have to go clean out the apartment tomorrow. We're going in the morning so I guess you can come when were done, because I'm sure no one wants to see you."

"Okay"

"You still have your key right?"

"Yeah".

"Okay I guess I'll call you tomorrow".

Chi Chi was all ears. I gave her a play by play then we called my daddy.

Sunday October 6th

Shelia called me repeatedly asking about various items in OUR house. This bitch just wanted to be in charge out of resentment of the situation. It didn't make any sense for her to be in the house without me. She knew nothing and a major fact of the matter was this, Teff had nothing but his clothes. EVERYTHING was mine! How do you say that shit to a grieving, guilt driven mother? Honestly, I didn't even have the strength to deal with this bullshit because the fact that I even had to do this shit was killing me inside. I was only physically there. I was in lala land and my phone was ringing back-to-back, from Shelia fishing to see what she can come up on from what she assumed was my lack of defense, followed by my daddy, my defense. As if that was not enough Saleena calls.

"Hey Nika, this Saleena"

"I know".

"I just wanna know what happened?

"What you mean?"

"I mean when I left his house from getting Miguel he was fine, what happened after I left? I mean did yall get into it or something?"

"Nothing happened".

"Well, you know Shelia calling me saying he didn't kill his self and your daddy did it."

"Something wrong with Shelia."

"Yeah, it is, well".

"Aight then."

Chi Chi was all ears. She was on my ass like white on rice.

"Who the fuck was that?"

"Saleena".

"What the fuck she want? See, give me your phone".

As soon as I handed it to her, it rang again.

"Hello, can I speak to Mr. Gonzalez".

You gotta be fucking kidding me I thought.

"This is his girlfriend".

"Well, I'm calling form Miguel B Lea Eros's office, were trying to cut him is check for his car accident".

"Well, he's dead".

There was a long silence as you could imagine.

"Oh wow,. ...okay, thank you".

Teff told me he had already gotten that check. Where did all the money come from he had that day? It didn't matter anymore. I was now pulling up in front of where we once lived and loved together, but I wasn't there to go home.

"Hey sis", my little brother greeted me as we parked.

I just smiled softly. I loved my baby Eric. Seeing his face usually made me feel good, but I was in so much pain I couldn't feel anything good.

"Aye, so we got the day bed, Symone bike and kitchen set, we know the pictures yours, you want the stuff in the refrigerator?

I just struggled my shoulders and laid my seat back so I could cry laying down.

I saw Chi Chi rolling up so I could attempt to digest the happenings of this day. Next thing you know my brother walks to the car with Teff's extra-large bottle of hot sauce. I lost it.

"NOOOOOOO!!!! Put it back, I don't want it! I wanna go, let's go Chi Chi".

I was crying hysterically. My dad ran to the car trying to figure out why I was screaming. Chi Chi had to explain how Teff loved hot sauce and that she was just going to take me back home. She handed him the keys to Teff's apartment. My daddy looked so helpless. He just stared at me.

"Baby girl I'm sorry, I didn't know". I just stared back at him.

"I love you, daddy loves you, Imma take this stuff to your apartment, just call me when you ready to talk. Aye, ya mom been wanting to talk to you but she say you not answering the phone."

I continued with my staring as I began to devour the blunt.

"Chi Chi, take care of my baby".

"You know I got Nika".

October 7-9th

As the days went by, I sank further into a depression. I did not eat, I barely slept, and I did not shower unless Chi Chi made me.

I suddenly had no desire for cigarettes anymore, which was weird because I loved my cigarettes, especially at a time like this. I still attempted to smoke them anyway because it was a habit and they usually would boost up my high, but they made me nauseous which did not help my already lost appetite.

Chi Chi continued trying to shove chicken nuggets down my throat. I had no desire to chew. My hunger pains didn't even bother me anymore because they were nothing compared to the pain in my heart.

The next few days were a blur. I continued to stay with Chi Chi and she hadn't left my side. Except for this one time, and she'll ever do it again because I went ballistic. I heard noises and I assumed it was Teff's ghost coming to kill because he hated me. When she came home, I was losing it. She promised to never leave me alone again. Poor Chi Chi, she was just trying to get her some.

Nothing got better as the days went on. Shelia continued to call me and say the most fucked up shit ever. Like, how they were still struggling with the money they needed to cremate him. I did not want him cremated. I felt like he would be able to feel it. I wanted him left alone. I wanted him to wake up. My dad advised me to find another apartment because it was clear that I would not return to the old one. Chi Chi looked around for me. I could not focus. I simply could not wrap my mind around the fact that I would never see him again. Why would he do this shit? Was my leaving that bad? Damn, I just needed to get away from him and all the drama, I never wanted this! All I did was think. I thought about every detail, every aspect, every second of the day. Weed just helped me not freak all the way out about my thoughts. I decided to make a doctor's appointment for no particular reason other than this seemed like a great time to confirm a great bill of health. Well, there was that one thing he said in the last message. You know, that, "Please don't kill my baby", part. It replayed in my mind. I had just taken a test last week and it said negative, but Teff insisted that it was incorrect. I had not even missed a period and I had no symptoms of such, but I needed to confirm.

I missed by baby. Chi Chi and I stopped over to my grandma's house to see her. My grandma was so blunt. She never held anything back. She said exactly what she wanted to say and never cared if it afflicted you. She did not give a shit. I hugged and kissed my baby, before I could bask in our reunion, I was interrupted by my grandmother's rudeness.

"So, when they go have that boy's funeral?"

Chi Chi and I flooded the room with our "Shhhhhhs" as I tried to quickly cover Symone's ears. I quickly escorted Symone into another room.

"Grandma, I don't want Symone to know what happened yet".

"Hell, she already know, she told me!"

Chi Chi and I stared at each other. How would she know? She was asleep when it happened. I never spoke of it in front of her, that was one of the reasons she was not with me at this time.

"Ask her, she already know. She said, "My daddy died".

I was devastated. My little pumpkin was too young to internalize something of this magnitude, she was only 4 years old. I had no idea what to say to her. Now I was even afraid to ask her what she wanted to eat. Chi Chi and I decided to take her to McDonalds for a happy meal and ice cream. I looked into the back seat at her beautiful innocent face.

"Symone, what you tell grandma about Teff? I cringed as I waited for her answer.

"I said, My daddy died, he's in the sky".

"Who told you that? How do you know that?"

"Because I saw him".

"Saw who baby?"

"My daddy"

I stared at Chi Chi as I grabbed a cigarette.

"Where you see him at?"

"He was talking to me, he said he okay mommy, he had on a merry soup."

I began to cry. I attempted to continue with my interrogation, but Chi Chi thoughtfully took over.

"Merry soup? Symone what's a Merry Soup?"

"It was lellow"

"The merry soup was lellow?"

"Yes."

I looked my baby dead in the face.

"Baby, what's a merry soup, what did it look like?"

"Like when you get Merried."

Chi Chi and I both let out a mutual "OOOOOH!!"

"A Married suit? Like the outfit a man wears when he gets married?"

"Yes, a merry soup! Don't cry mommy, he's okay, he said he loves you, he told me to take care of you cause he's in the sky".

I continued to cry. I was so full of emotions. Terrified, heartbroken, creeped out and somehow relieved. She could not have made this up, she was too young to even think of such a lie. So, he talked to my baby, why didn't he talk to me? Is it because he hated me? Well, he said he loved me and for her to take care of me, that did not seem like hate. Now my brain was on overload again, not to mention the cigarette had made me feel worse. Shelia had called me on the way over to see Symone and said that tomorrow the family was going over to the funeral home to view his body before the cremation. She also mentioned two more disturbing things as if this alone wasn't disturbing enough.

"The family hates you and no one wants to see you, but you are welcomed to come".

"They're not going to fix him up too much because he's getting cremated, so I don't know if his brains are blown out or what."

Great, thanks Shelia.

I took Symone back inside and explained that Teffs "Funeral" was tomorrow, and I'd be back for Symone in a few days.

CHAPTER 13

WHAT NOW?
October 10th, 2002

My doctor's appointment was at 10:30 am. Chi Chi did not want to get up to take me, so I drove her car because I had given my car away to her cousin Courtney. She just asked if she could drive it, I told her to keep the muthafucker. I didn't want to have anything to do with it. Everything about it reminded me of Teff. Hell, I never drove it, Teff chauffeured me around in it. It still had his blood stains in it from when he got shot. His hub caps were on it and his entire music system. The last time I saw him alive I was sitting in it. Fuck that car.

I was afraid to listen to music and I was afraid to ride in silence. What if one of our songs came on? I decided on silence and weed.

"What brings you in today? Are you having any issues?"

"Check me for everything".

"Okay, so you want a full std screening?

"Yes."

"Syphilis and aids?"

"Yes."

"Pregnancy test?"

"Yes."

I sat on the table in my paper gown thinking, "What if he had Aids. What if he killed his self because he had given me some God-awful disease and now, I'm stuck with it". Before I could drown deeper in my thoughts.

"Ms. Jones."

I gave the doctor and nurse my deep stare I'd become so good at.

"Well, good news! Your std free. You can call this number to get the results for the Aids and syphilis in 7 days"

I began to breathe again.

"Oh, but there's one more thing."

Stare.

"You're pregnant" he said with so much excitement.

I almost fell off the table with tears. The nurse quickly ran over to comfort me. Confusion covered both of their faces.

"Is it a bad time for a pregnancy?"

"My boyfriend killed his self-Thursday"

They both grabbed me and handed me tissues. Before I knew it the entire staff was in my room. They gave a referral to see a psychiatrist. I just wanted to get the fuck out of there. The drive home was a blur. I tossed the remainder of my pack of cigarettes out of the window. I walked into Chi Chis apartment and blurted out;

"I'm pregnant", then tossed her the keys.

"You gotta be fucking kidding me!"

Stare.

"Welp, let's go."

It was 11:30 a.m. Teffs' viewing was at 12. Perfect timing.

I was literally shaking. We passed the funeral home and parked at a nearby corner store. I was losing it. I was petrified. Not only was I about to see my dead boyfriend whose death was all my fault. His angry grieving family were waiting to hate me in person. I am pregnant, and no one knew, and I wasn't sure if my now baby daddy's brains would be splattered everywhere as Shelia so politely added to my already irrational thoughts. I was not sure if today was the worst day of my life or the day Teff actually died. I wanted to run and hide. Did I have to do this? Would I regret it if I said fuck all of this madness and did not say goodbye. Can you really say goodbye to someone who was already gone? Was it worth it? What if I passed out? What if I walked in and Saleena tried to fight me? My head was spinning. Chi Chi convinced me that everything would be fine.

"Ain't nobody go try you! I'll beat Shelia's AND Saleena's ass!"

I'm scared to see him Chi Chi", I cried like a baby.

"Imma go look at him first, if I can't take it, I won't let you see him."

I knew she meant it. It gave me a lot of comfort. I hit the blunt a few more times as we pulled in. I felt like my legs would give out as we walked up to the door. I took a deep breath as we entered the funeral home. The entire family turned and looked at us as we entered. Their faces bawled up and they rolled their eyes at my very sight. Saleena's dramatic ass let out a sigh that blew my hair, and I didn't have any. Stupid bitch. The family didn't like her either, they just liked her more than me, today. Chi Chi and I just stood in our little corner. No one acknowledged me. Shelia had been halfway cordial to me over the phone but I guess she was in her feelings today so she couldn't let her family see her being nice to me. Fine. I just wanted this shit to be over so I could get back in Chi Chi's bed to cry and absorb the fact that I now had a baby Teff inside my body, and I did not know if I loved it or hated it.

The funeral home man came out to greet us and explained that the visit had begun. I watched as His uncle, brothers, Saleena and Shelia all walked in the room one by one and in small groups and walked back out crying. It was terrible, sad and scary. Were they crying because he was dead, and they missed him, or did he look that terrible? The wait was agonizing.

Finally, it was our turn. Chi Chi and I walked up to the door together. I stopped and Chi Chi continued directly into the room and up to his body. I saw the top of his head and his hand that rested outside of the white sheet he was covered in. Chi Chi jumped. Oh my God, was it like a crime scene? Was it too late for me to run out? In the middle of me freaking out, Chi Chi reached her hand out. I stared at it for a few seconds before I walked toward it. I focused on walking toward the hand. I held it tightly as I turned around and slowly open my eyes. There he was. My baby, the man I slept with every night, the man I loved. Lifeless.

Dead. Darker. Hard. There was a gauze bandage over each temple. His mouth was slightly open, and his teeth were biting down. His hand was still in the shape of the gun. I burst into tears. I wanted him to get up! I was sorry! I was just scared of him. I mean I knew he wouldn't hurt me on purpose. I knew he loved me but, sometimes I didn't know what he may have been capable of. I had to go, I just had too. Things were too bad, I was miserable. What was I to do? I never thought this would happen. I just thought, we would just, break up. Never this.

"I'm sorry I didn't believe you. I love you so much. We go have a baby."

I heard Shelia sign loudly in response.

I needed to get the fuck out of there. That was enough for today. Just as I made it out of the door Shelia stopped us.

"Nika, you pregnant?" she asked with excitement in her voice.

"Yes ma'am."

"Wow, that's the circle of life. If you have the baby, I'll do whatever I can for the baby. If you don't have the baby, I can't have anything to do with that."

"I don't know. I don't know what Imma do, I just found out today. This is a lot. I don't think I can do this."

To be continued....

CONCLUSION

Never stay in a situation where you must run to feel safe. Love is blind, but signs are everywhere. Missing a sign could sometimes mean life or death. Mental illness is real. Suicide is real. If you need help, find it. Sometimes your worse enemy can be that voice in your head. Telling you, you are not good enough. Telling you that you do not deserve something wonderful or even that you do deserve something horrible. Or that that horrible thing that happened TO YOU, is your fault. Tell that voice to shut the fuck up! Tell that voice, the truth, and that is;

Yes, I have made some mistakes and I may have been put in circumstances that were out of my control at the time. That does not change the fact that I am here for a reason. I am not perfect, but I am NOT my circumstances. I am me, and no matter who does or does not love me, I love me. I will not hurt me.

AIN'T NO FIRE EVER BURNED ME, IT ONLY REFINED ME, BECAUSE THAT IS WHAT I DECIDED. YOU GET TO DECIDE. EVEN WHEN YOU DO NOT GET TO DECIDE, YOU GET TO DECIDE.

Thank you for reading my book. I have struggled with this book for at least 10 years. So many tears went into this book. I am crying now, but finally, tears of joy. It means everything to release this very real story. I have so much more to say. This is book number 1 of my 7-book series. I am inviting you join me for this ride. It will be worth every line, trust me.

Please follow me on my social media outlets and visit my website to stay tuned for release dates, blogs, book signings and so much more!

www.NikaJ.xyz

DEDICATION

This book is dedicated to my beautiful middle child Ymani D..

In this book, you will read things you have never heard before. I held a lot of facts from you to protect you. Sometimes, the truth hurts, but just know;

You are my gift left by the love of my life. You were made from love. I love you, there is no one like you. My diamond out of the rough. Through the fire....

ACKNOWLEDGEMENTS

I would thank the following people....

- Ebony N. Wilson for make-up.

- Porsha Harris (Express Press Hair Care) for Hair.

- Lauren Hatchett for Photography.

- Alice Simpson for editing.

- Kisha Carmichael-Motley for editing and direction.

- Avis Fields for support and Foreword

- Australia Miller for book cover design.

I would like to also thank all of my family and friends for dealing with my crazy ass. I love ya'll.

JG4 Life

WWW.NIKAJ.XYZ